An introduction to excellence in practice development in health and social care

An introduction to excellence in practice development in health and social care

Rob McSherry and Jerry Warr

 Open University Press

Open University Press
McGraw-Hill Education
McGraw-Hill House
Shoppenhangers Road
Maidenhead
Berkshire
England
SL6 2QL

email: enquiries@openup.co.uk
world wide web: www.openup.co.uk

and Two Penn Plaza, New York, NY 10121-2289, USA

First published 2008

A catalogue record of this book is available from the British Library

ISBN-13: 978 0 335 22321 3 (pb)   978 0 335 22322 0 (hb)
ISBN-1: 0-335-22321-4 (pb)   0-335-22322-2 (hb)

Library of Congress Cataloging-in-Publication Data
CIP data applied for

Typeset by RefineCatch Limited, Bungay, Suffolk
Printed in Great Britain by Bell and Bain Ltd., Glasgow

The *McGraw·Hill* Companies

Contents

Introducing the series   vi

1   Introducing practice development to facilitate excellence in care   1
2   The drivers for excellence in health and social care   32
3   Excellence in context: contemporary health and social care   46
4   Changing organisational cultures and working environments   60
5   Care standards and organisational accreditation schemes   79
6   Practical approaches to developing excellence in care in oneself   95
7   The way forward to achieving excellence in care through
    practice development   120

Index   129

Introducing the series: Excellence in practice development in health and social care'

The aim of this book *'An introduction to excellence in practice development in health and social care'* and series *'Excellence in practice development in health and social care'* is to provide the reader with the underlying principles and techniques to foster excellence in practice in any health and social care setting. The emphasis of the series and text will not focus on specific health: National Health Service (NHS) – Acute Hospital Trusts, Foundation Trusts, Primary Care Trusts, or Social Care: Children's Trusts, Residential or Care Home settings but will outline how the principles and techniques of Practice Development (PD) can support innovation, change and excellence within them. Practice development is a "term used to describe particular approaches to supporting change in health care (predominately nursing) for over 20 years" (McCormack et al 2006). Over the past couple of years it has been acknowledged that the philosophy, principles, tools and techniques associated with PD are relevant to all professional and non-professional bodies, teams and organisations working within health and social care sectors (McSherry & Warr 2006, McCormack et al 2006). Throughout the texts the authors will refer to 'care' which incorporates both health and social care settings using examples to reinforce debate or discussion. Whether you are a registered professional: nurse, general practitioner, social worker, occupational therapist, physiotherapists, dentist, pharmacist, optometrist or a non-registered professional: healthcare support worker, occupational therapy support worker, home care or residential support worker or managers and leaders the series and text will be relevant to you and your practice setting.

So what is the reason for putting this series of books together?

Firstly, the introduction and establishment of health and social care accreditation schemes and standards by the Health Care Commission (HC) or Social Care Institute for Excellence (SCIE) (to name but two) has posed challenges and difficulties for individuals, teams and organisations to provide the evidence to demonstrate an acquired level of excellence in practice. The way forward for staff working in practice is to view health and social care standards and accreditation as an opportunity rather than a threat to practice. The dilemma for health and social care professionals and non-professionals working in practice is in accessing a framework(s) or tools and techniques to support them in developing excellence rather than contributing to stress and anxiety in the workforce.

Secondly, it is imperative that the HC and SCIE along with other accrediting bodies use their authority to encourage all inspectorates to unite. Unification of the various organisational accrediting bodies is imperative. The key disadvantages of organisational standards and accreditation within the health and social care today is in the duplication of time, resources and support needed for individuals, teams and organisations in collecting, collating and providing the evidence to meet the required standard(s).

Thirdly, health and social care organisations according to McSherry et al. (2004) seem to be pressurised not just in meeting the criteria for one award but several at any one time. A critical review of the organisational and accreditation frameworks such as Healthcare Commission (HC), Social Care Institute for Excellence (SCIE), Investors in People (IIP), European Foundation Quality Management (EFQM), Clinical Negligence Scheme for Trusts (CNST) and Charter Mark (CM) has already revealed a set of primary core themes in the publication of the Excellence in Practice Accreditation Scheme (EPAS) (McSherry et al, 2003). From our experiences of working with registered and non-registered professionals and teams from across a diverse range of specialities and organisations they lack time, support, resources and investment to review and improve standards of care. Pugh et al. (2005) and Hoban (2007) like McSherry et al (2003: 627) demonstrate that EPAS "provides a robust framework supporting the clinical governance agenda, as the main themes from EPAS clearly match the themes from the clinical governance agenda". Clinical governance according to Stanton (2007: viii) is

> "not, and has never been, an end in itself. Alongside effective financial and general management it is one essential means to the promotion of sustained quality in the care provided by individual healthcare staff, by teams, by organisations and by a co-ordinated and coherent local health and social care system".

There are many examples of organisational accreditation schemes but none of them fully capture the essence of clinical governance or evidence-based practice within a practice development framework. The uniqueness of the EPAS is in collectively addressing the key issues in developing, advancing and evaluating practice, which could easily be transferred and further, developed to incorporate the non-clinical aspects of an integrated governance model and health and social care standards.

Fourthly, in an attempt to address the challenges and difficulties associated with health and social accreditation schemes to demonstrate a desired standard of care and to be proactive in tackling the political, professional and public expectations for providing world class health and social care. The editors and contributors to the series believed that there was a need to offer professionals and non-professionals working in health and social care a series of texts that provide simple and effective tools and techniques to support the development of excellence in practice. Each text contains a combination of activities, case studies and reflective questions, along with a summary of key points, recommended reading and useful resources to build confidence and competence to innovate and change either individual, team and organisational practice. The series of texts should appeal because of the fact that the experts themselves from a diverse range of specialities, professional backgrounds and different parts of the United Kingdom (UK) will be writing and sharing experiences within the texts.

References

Hoben, V. (2007) Is practice development under threat? *Nursing Times* 103(24): 16–18.

McCormack, B., Dewar, B., Wright, J., Garbett, R., Harvey, G., Ballantine, K. (2006) *A realist synthesis of evidence relating to practice development*; Executive summary NHS Quality Improvement Sotland and NHS Education for Scotland, Scotland.

McSherry, R., Kell, J., Mudd, D. (2003) Practice Development: best practice using Excellence in Practice Accreditation Scheme. *British Journal of Nursing* 12(10): 623–629.

McSherry, R., Warr, J. (2006) Practice development: confirming the existence of a knowledge and evidence base. *Practice Development in Health Care* 5(2): 55–79.

Pugh, E., Lockey, M., McSherry, R., Mudd, D. (2005) Creating order out of chaos: Towards excellence in practice. *Practice Development in Health Care* 4(3): 138–141.

Stanton, A.P. (2007) Forward in: McSherry, R., Pearce, P. (2007) *Clinical Governance A Guide to Implementation for Healthcare Professionals* 2nd Edn, Blackwell Publishing, London.

Introducing practice development to facilitate excellence in care

Introduction

This chapter briefly outlines the drivers for practice development and excellence in practice followed by a detailed outline of what the terms and phrases mean and how this can be facilitated in practice. This is achieved by exploring the key characteristics and qualities required to take practice development forward along with outlining some of the tools and techniques to aid the process.

Background

The rationale for the introduction of phrases or terms like: evidence-based practice, clinical governance, practice development and excellence in practice, according to Pickering & Thompson (2003), could be attributed to a perceived decline in the standards and quality of care provision. This is because all of these phrases or terms are directly and or indirectly focused on promoting individuals, teams and organisations in the delivery of quality care and services. This point is confirmed by McSherry & Pearce (2007) arguing that the origins for developing quality health and social care services arise from a combination of societal, political and professional factors such as the following:

- rising patient/client and carer expectation
- increased dependency of those accessing services
- technological advances
- demographic changes in society
- changes in care delivery systems
- lack of public confidence in healthcare services
- threat of litigation
- demands for greater access to information.

To address and respond to the growing pressures to change, reform or modernise to keep up with the times, it is important that health and social care professionals recognise what, why and how practice development may aid the pursuit of excellence in practice. In order for this to happen it is imperative that we understand what we mean by the terms practice development and excellence in practice.

What do we mean by practice development and excellence in practice?

Over the past decade Page & Hamer (2002) argue that the term practice development (PD) has been associated with supporting modernisation, and organisational, service and quality improvements but more importantly in promoting patient centredness (McCormack et al., 1999). Promoting patient-centred care as advocated by McCormack et al. (1999) could arguably be seen as the kingpin of excellence, as without achieving this could we claim to be providing quality care and/or services? The perceived value of practice development in promoting excellence in practice according to Elwyn (1998) and McSherry & Bassett (2002) is linked to its facilitative approach to engaging patients and users with change and innovation through collaboration, team working and partnership building. Glover (1998; 2002) and McSherry & Driscoll (2004) argue that despite the plethora of literature outlining the relative strengths and weaknesses of practice development to the health and social care professions, professionals, and health and social care organisations, there is limited evidence available substantiating the existence of a knowledge base within the field of practice development and whether it improves or promotes excellence in practice.

Activity 1.1 Reflective question

Write down what you understand by the terms practice development and excellence in practice.

Read on and compare your notes with the activity feedback at the end of the chapter.

What is practice development and how can it facilitate excellence?

In order to understand why and how practice development can facilitate excellence in practice it is imperative to know where the term originated and what it means. The next section is adapted from the working McSherry & Warr (2006).

Practice development – a brief historical overview

Practice development, according to McSherry & Warr (2006), was primarily introduced into the UK by the nursing profession in the late 1970s and early 1980s during a major transitional and reforming period. Nursing at the time was shifting from a traditionalist approach to practice based on tasks, rituals and the division of labour (skill-mix and profiling) towards a patient-centred approach based on quality, standards, education and evaluation (McCormack et al., 1999). Essentially nursing (through practice development) was trying to break free from the chains of medicine, managerialism and the hierarchy of routines for a professionalism based on providing individualised patient-centred care through the execution of independent accountable and autonomous decision-making and practice (Glover, 2002). The quest for independent, accountable and autonomous decision-making in practice produced an intensity of activity within the field of practice development. Activities have ranged from the introduction of Nurse Development (Lathan & Vaughan, 1997) and Practice Development Units (Page et al., 1998), the establishment of individuals and teams with a remit for practice development (Bassett, 1996; Glover, 2002), the development of a national Practice Development Forum (Mallett, 2000) (known today as The Developing Practice Subscribers Area with Foundation of Nursing Studies (FONS)) and ongoing research and development into practice development to name but a few (Taylor et al., 2002).

Practice development, and methodologies to support it, have been discussed in international literature. In Australia, the literature has emphasised its role as a catalyst for change (Walker, 2003) and the role of facilitating teams to effect change (Walsh et al., 2004). In the USA, Haag-Heitman & Kramer (1998) have proposed a clinical practice development model and Cambron & Cain (2004) suggest that there are lessons to learn from the UK movement. The term 'practice development' appears in the literature of other countries occasionally (e.g. Pitkanen et al., 2004), but there is an increasing emphasis on related concepts and alternative phrases (Wong, 2002: Gustafsson & Fargerberg, 2004).

Practice development is an approach that recognises the realities of external influence whilst allowing an individual service to focus on developing excellence in practice in all areas. It is an inclusive 'bottom up' approach to review and change the whole service which puts the patient at the centre of the care process. It has many definitions which emphasise different aspects of these qualities but one we have found useful by exploring the literature and for practical delivery and which will be developed further in this and subsequent books is:

> Practice development's primary principles are centred on promoting patient-centredness through the utilisation of a facilitative approach to team working, collaboration and partnership building (McSherry & Warr, 2006:75).

This facilitative approach to innovation and change offers an ideal vehicle to utilise targets and standards through an inclusive and empowering way to develop local practice. As such, targets have a central role in promoting excellence through practice development (Figure 1.1).

Despite the potential benefits of practice development in promoting excellence it is imperative that individuals, teams and organisations understand what the term means.

- Give direction
- Allow benchmarking
- Stimulate improvement
- Foster audit and research
- Aid team approaches
- Engage users of the service
- Support innovation and change
- Provide tools and techniques to enhance change
- Enhance the working environment and culture of the organisation
- Offer a vehicle for sharing, disseminating and networking
- Demonstrate impact of change

Figure 1.1 Targets in practice development

Defining practice development

The term *practice development* has been defined and conceptualised over the past two decades resulting in numerous definitions (Figure 1.2) attempting to decipher what it means and involves. Practice development according to Kitson (1994:319) can best be described as:

> a system whereby identified or appointed change agents work with staff to help them introduce a new activity or practice. The findings may come from the findings of rigorous research; findings of less rigorous research; experience which has not been tested systematically or trying out an idea in practice. The introduction of the development ought to be systematic and carefully evaluated to ensure that the new practice has achieved improvement intended.

What Kitson's (1994) definition highlights is the importance research plays in driving change and that the proposed change may prove or disprove the research theory. It could also be inferred that practice development supports the government's drive for a more systematic and rigorous approach to NHS research and development through focusing attention on the implementation and utilisation of research findings in practice. In contrast to Kitson's (1994) definition, Mallett et al. (1997) introduced the notion that practice development should be based on patients' needs by arguing the case that practice and professional development, although viewed synonymously at times, were distinctively different. This point was endorsed by McCormack & Garbett (2003) who suggest professional development refers to developing the knowledge and skills of the individual whilst practice development is about creating optimal organisational cultures and working environments to aid individuals in applying such skills. By exploring the definitions and distinctions between practice and professional development at best practice development should be defined as:

> continuous process of improvement towards increased effectiveness in person-centered care, through the enabling of nurses and health care

teams to transform the culture and context of care. It is enabled and supported by facilitators committed to a systematic, rigorous and continuous process of emancipatory change (McCormack et al., 1999:258).

Furthermore, taking a critical review of Kitson's (1994), Mallet et al.'s (1997) and McCormack et al.'s (1999) definitions of practice development reveals that the role of practice development is that of facilitator in supporting the creation of optimal cultures and contexts to promote innovation and changes in practice. Practice development is about encouraging individuals, teams and organisations to improve practice through innovation and change (McSherry & Bassett, 2002). Practice development plays a pivotal role in fostering a culture and context that nurtures evidence-based nursing because it is an:

approach that synthesises activities and theory of quality improvement, evidence-base and innovations in practice, within a real-practice context, and with a central focus on the improvement of care and services for patients and clients (Page & Hammer, 2002:6).

Similarly practice development is distinctive and unique because it happens within the professional's 'own' practice setting and is about the enhancement and growth of personal, professional and/or organisational standards and quality of services by involving and focusing on the patients' and clients' specific needs.

Excellence in practice requires team-working, interdisciplinary collaboration, effective communication, internal and external partnerships and a willingness to learn and share with and from each other; including users of the NHS (McSherry, 2004:140).

To achieve the status of being an effective individual, team and organisation, practice development requires support, investment and most importantly recognition from health and social care professionals themselves; recognition that practice development is an integral part of all of our roles and everyone's responsibility to advance and evaluate practice. The fundamental aim of practice development is

to act in partnership, providing support between clinical practice, education and management, enabling them to increase research utilisation (Bassett, 1996:18).

Taking the above definitions and those summarised in Figure 1.1 along with the emerging debates about what practice development is and means, it could be argued that practice development is ideal in promoting quality improvements in care . . . as well as one's self! (McSherry & Driscoll (2004.)) This is because practice development is pertinent to all health and social care professionals, teams and organisations.

A critical review of the definitions provided in Figure 1.2 and exploring the work of O'Neal & Manley (2007), McCormack et al. (2006), McSherry & Warr (2006), along with *A Strategy for Practice Development* (Health Service

Author: Kitson
Year: 1994
Definition: A system whereby identified or appointed change agents work with staff to help them introduce a new activity or practice. The findings may come from the findings of rigorous research; findings of less rigorous research; experience which has not been tested systematically or trying out an idea in practice. The introduction of the development ought to be systematic and carefully evaluated to ensure that the new practice has achieved improvement intended.
Key themes derived from definition:
• Change
• Research
• Experience
• Systematic
• Evaluation
• Improvement

Author: Bassett
Year: 1994
Definition: Practice development is to act in partnership, providing support between clinical practice, education and management, enabling them to increase research utilisation.
Key themes derived from definition:
• Partnership
• Support
• Enabling
• Evidence

Author: McCormack et al.
Year: 1999
Definition: Continuous process of improvement towards increased effectiveness in person-centred care, through the enabling of nurses and health care teams to transform the culture and context of care. It is enabled and supported by facilitators committed to a systematic, rigorous and continuous process of emancipatory change.
Key themes derived from definition:
• Continuous
• Quality
• Person-centred
• Enabling
• Working environment
• Culture
• Systematic process
• Facilitation

Author: Clarke & Wilcockson
Year: 2001
Definition: The ways in which practitioners engage with and create knowledge with which they effect development in their understanding and practice of patient care.
Key themes derived from definition:
• Engage
• Knowledge
• Quality
• Patient-centred

Author: McSherry & Bassett
Year: 2002
Definition: Practice development is about encouraging individuals, teams and organisations to improve practice through innovation and change.

Key themes derived from definition:
• Encouraging
• Innovation
• Change

Author: Page & Hamer
Year: 2002
Definition: Approach that synthesises activities and theory of quality improvement, evidence-based and innovations in practice, within a real-practice context, and with a central focus on the improvement of care and services for patients and clients.
Key themes derived from definition:
• Systematic approach
• Patient-centred
• Evidence
• Facilitation
• Change

Author: Garbett & McCormack
Year: 2002
Definition: A process of increased effectiveness in person-centred care.
Key themes derived from definition:
• Process
• Systematic
• Person centred

Author: McSherry
Year: 2004
Definition: About encouraging and motivating staff to innovate or evaluate practices, regardless of size, in the quest for improved quality.
Key themes derived from definition:
• Encouraging
• Motivation
• Quality

Author: Hynes
Year: 2004
Definition: Questioning practice in the context of evidence to support what it is we, as practitioners, do, why we do it so, and how it can be done differently.
Key themes derived from definition:
• Challenging
• Evidence
• Quality

Author: McSherry & Warr
Year: 2006
Definition: Practice development's primary principles are centred on promoting patient centredness through the utilisation of a facilitative approach to team working, collaboration and partnership building.
Key themes derived from definition:
• Patient centredness
• Facilitation
• Change
• Collaboration
• Partnerships

Figure 1.2 A critical review of practice development definitions

Executive Southern Ireland, 2007) reveals an interesting and useful framework encapsulating key themes about what practice development is and how it can facilitate excellence in practice (Figure 1.3).

Figure 1.3 depicts how practice development is about encouraging (McSherry & Bassett, 2002), enabling (Bassett, 1996; McCormack et al., 1999), engaging (Clarke & Wilcockson, 2001) and enlightening (McSherry & Warr, 2006) individuals, teams and organisations to rise to the challenges and demands placed on health and social care services to change and keep up with the times. Practice development is ideal in supporting innovation and change by offering a continuous systematic framework/process for facilitating the advancement and evaluation of individual, team and organisational practice(s) (Kitson, 1994; McCormack et al., 1999; Garbett & McCormack,

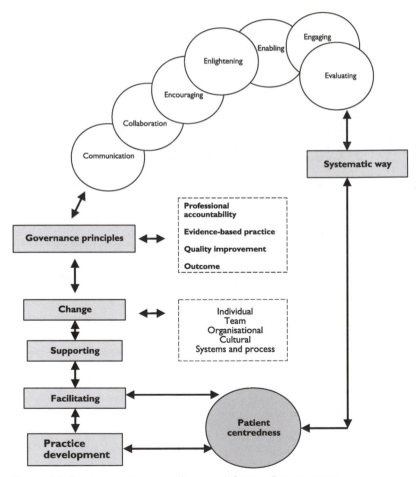

Figure 1.3 Practice development: a framework for excellence in practice

2002; Page & Hamer 2002). Ultimately the purpose of practice development is about ensuring that person/patient centredness (McCormack et al., 1999; Clarke & Wilcockson, 2001; Garbett & McCormack, 2002; Page & Hamer, 2002; McSherry & Warr, 2006) is at the heart of all innovation and change. User involvement in care delivery and evaluation is imperative in order to bring about continuous quality (Clarke & Wilcockson, 2001; McSherry & Bassett, 2002; Hynes, 2004) and or service improvements (Kitson et al., 1994) within the context of governance principles (McSherry, 2004). Governance principles are based on ensuring that every health and social care professional and worker focuses on promoting person/patient-centred care through:

- developing knowledge, skills and competency as part of their professional accountability and roles and responsibilities outlined in their job description
- ensuring they support their decision and actions with appropriate evidence.

Similarly, practice development is about generating evidence from practice in order to inform future innovation and change through:

- focusing on providing and developing quality care and services with users and providers of the service
- introducing ways to capture, measure and demonstrate the impact of change on the patient, service or clinical outcome or the efficiency and effectiveness of the change on individuals, teams and organisations
- having the backing of the organisation to offer education and training to support innovation and change.

The value of practice development in promoting governance principles is the fact that it 'draws on many different and diverse disciplines, which in turn enables all professionals to be integrated for the benefit of patients' (McCormack et al., 2002:35). Practice development is about enabling health and social care workers, teams and organisations to transform the culture and context in which care is provided. In order to achieve this Bassett (1996) argues it is about developing partnerships, providing support between clinical practice, education and management, enabling them to increase research utilisation. This can only be achieved successfully, according to McSherry (1999), through developing:

- **Team work**: between all key stakeholders (including users and carers) within and external to the team.
- **Multi-professional collaboration**: Involving the multi-disciplinary team members including ancillary team members.
- **Effective communication**: between, within and across all the stakeholders involved with the innovation and change.

Manley & McCormack (2003:23) argue that the 'raison d'être of practice development is to improve some aspect of patient care or service directly', regardless of the methodologies used, or the assumptions, beliefs and values held. To this end Manley & McCormack (2003) and McCormack et al. (2002) illustrate why and how practice development eloquently links to Habermas's (1972) critical social theory/science.

Critical social theory or science as it is often referred

> is used as a generic term to describe the attempt to theorise the modern social world in any of its spheres (the psychological, the cultural, the economic, the legal, or the political), then 'critical social theory' means firstly, social theory which is capable of taking a critical stance towards itself, by recognising its own presuppositions and its own role in the social world, and secondly, social theory which takes a critical stance towards the social reality that it investigates, by providing grounds for the justification and criticism of the institutions, practices and mentalities that make up that reality (Yacopeth, 2007).

Put simply critical social theory as described by Habermas (1972) is about exploring the world we live in and the structures and systems within it and around it. Critical social theory is a philosophy well suited for practice development because it is

> a means to frame enquiry, with the aim of liberating groups from constraints (either conscious or unconscious) that interfere with balanced participation in social interaction (Mooney & Nolan, 2006:241).

This notion of liberation and balanced participation is important within practice development because change and innovation is directly and indirectly linked to the identification of assumptions, values and belief. 'Assumptions are usually unconscious, but by making assumptions conscious, explicit values and beliefs can be articulated' (McCormack et al., 2002). Mooney & Nolan (2006) added clarity to the debate surrounding assumptions, values and beliefs by arguing that society is structured by rules, habits, convictions and meanings to which people follow. The notion of liberation and balanced participation is important in practice development because it is about attempting to encourage, empower and engage individuals, teams and organisations through dynamic management and leadership in the quest to improve patient care and/or services. To bring about these types of changes may or may not require a development in self-awareness and knowledge along with a challenge to existing assumptions, values and beliefs held by individuals, teams and organisations. This idea of knowledge is an important factor associated with critical social theory and practice development because by adopting an orientation towards critical praxis that is synchronised reflection and action, we hope to facilitate a review of what knowledge is, the way in which one comes to know and those who provide knowledge (Habermas, 1972; Mooney & Nolan, 2006). McCormack et al. (2002) and Manley & McCormack (2003) expand the different kinds of knowledge debate and how knowledge can be realised within practice development in three ways: technical, practical and emancipatory (Figure 1.4).

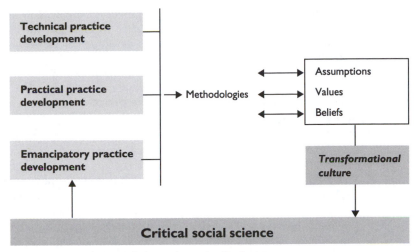

Figure 1.4 Types of knowledge and practice development

Figure 1.4 simply and briefly illustrates how critical social theory or science as a philosophy supports practice development by focusing attention on enhancing three types of knowledge: technical – concerned with enhancing knowledge that will improve skills, competency akin to science such as pain relief, wound care and management; practical – associated with understanding what others know and feel about the care or service received; emancipatory – focuses on self-awareness and reflection and how the individual influences or is influenced by the working environment, culture and context in which they work. It is about empowering and disempowering others and its influence on innovation and change. Practice development is about focusing attention on enhancing these types of knowledge through using one or several methodologies, for example, engaging the research process to review or evaluate a given situation that results in a shift or change in the assumptions, beliefs and values held, thus bringing about a change in culture and context for the given situation. For more information on critical social theory/science and practice development see Box 1.

Box 1.1 Critical social theory/science and practice development

More detailed information about critical social theory/science and practice development can be found in the following publications:

McCormack, B., Manley, K., Garbett, R. (2004) *Practice Development in Nursing.* Blackwell Science: Oxford.
Manley, K., McCormack, B. (2003) Practice development: purpose, methodology, facilitation and evaluation. *Nursing in Critical Care* 8(1): 22–9.

Having identified what practice development is along with its underpinning philosophical foundations it is imperative to highlight the characteristics and qualities required to take practice development forward in any given health and social care setting.

Characteristics and qualities required to take practice development forward

A description of the characteristics, qualities and skills in practice development based on the work of McCormack & Garbett (2003) outlined in Figure 1.5 reveals that the characteristics and qualities of practice developers is about encouraging and motivating staff to innovate or evaluate practices regardless of size of the project in the quest for improved quality. Successful practice development is dependent upon encouraging and supporting individuals to develop certain essential skills and attributes so that they can advance and/or evaluate practice as part of the change processes.

A review of the characteristics and qualities of the work of McCormack & Garbett (2003) along with the works of McSherry & Bassett (2002) and McSherry & Driscoll (2004) highlighted in Box 1.2 reveals several key qualities and individual personal attributes that seem to make practice development occur. For practice development to occur a blend of the essential qualities and individual personal attributes are required within the process of change.

Box 1.2 Essential and individual attributes associated with practice development

Commitment	Motivate
Respect	Facilitate
Experience	Innovate
Approachable	Inform
An agent of change	Encourage
Supportive	Support

For some health and social care organisations, practice development facilitators, advisers or developers are available to support and facilitate change. However, for other organisations and individuals this is not the case, placing pressure on individuals and teams to take responsibility for advancing and evaluating their own or team's practice as part of an ever-changing agenda. The introduction of named 'practice developers' is essential if health and social care organisations and teams are to modernise within busy, stressful and time-pressured practice areas. Several models have been reported and commented upon which could be used as exemplars in developing these posts further within the NHS (Glover, 2002). It is also worth considering the

Characteristics
- *Promoting and facilitating change* – supporting individuals, teams or larger groups in the organisation to create a culture in which to support change based on the needs of those practitioners directly involved with such change
- *Translation and communication* – often being situated between 'top management' and the practice arena means helping staff interpret as well as disseminate policy documents and information from 'top down' or generating interest for change at a local level from 'bottom up'
- *Responding to external influences* – helping shape or 'set the agenda' for specific work being undertaken in practice based on policy or professional documents
- *Education* – providing both formal and informal access to personal and professional development for qualified staff in order to manage change
- *Research into practice* – disseminating findings and best practice(s) in relation to change being considered
- *Audit and quality (including the development of policies and guidelines)* – working with staff teams and organisations to formally develop best practice(s) and measure the effects in practice

Qualities
- *Affective* – energy, enthusiasm, optimism and having a positive outlook
- *Having vision* – to underpin practice development activities concerned with bringing about improvements in patient/service user care
- *Being motivated* – having the necessary enthusiasm to enable change to happen
- *Being empathic* – understanding how the nature of change impacts on everyday practice
- *Experiential* – the ability to process personally and learn by going through the experience of change often though formal clinical supervision relationships

Skills
- *Cognitive* – the need to be creative in problem solving including effective ways of communicating with others about practice development and in finding resources
- *Political awareness* – working 'in the middle' through having access to senior management whilst also working with practitioners in their everyday work
- *Communicative* – being able to acquire and process information and articulate arguments for change in practice
- *Facilitative* – enabling others to reflect on practice with the intention of articulating, developing and more importantly acting on their ideas leading to change
- *Clinical* – viewed as being 'clinically credible' with peers without which practice development activities and change would be more difficult to achieve

Figure 1.5 A description of the characteristics, qualities and skills in practice development (based on McCormack & Garbett, 2003)

importance of ensuring that the introduction of new practice development positions are not tied in with other aspects of the governance agenda because this makes the posts too big and difficult to operationalise successfully (Garbett & McCormack, 2001). To meet the health and social modernisation agendas it could be easy to say that all health and social care professionals have or should possess the skills outlined in Figure 1.5 and Box 1.2. However, within practice development they become even more important when facilitating the development and evaluation of new or existing ways of working. To advance and evaluate practice within the context of health and social care it is imperative for individuals and teams to be familiar with the various tools and techniques to aid the process of change.

Tools and techniques to aid practice development within the context of health and social care

This section defines facilitation along with relating this important term to practice development. The section then goes on to provide several individual, team and organisational tools and techniques that may support the advancement and evaluation in practice.

Facilitation – its importance to achieving excellence in practice

Facilitation is undoubtedly an important factor for effective practice development and is an essential concept to understand in relation to supporting innovation and change. Simmons (2004) argues that facilitation is a widely used concept within health and social care, for example psychology (Burke et al., 2000), social care (Hunter et al., 1996), education (Cross, 1996) and research (Soltis-Jarrett, 1997) to name but a few. Generally facilitation is defined as 'to make easy or easier' (Collins, 1987:308). Facilitation within the context of practice development is more difficult and challenging to define because it is poorly articulated and understood (Simmons, 2004). At best practice development 'facilitation' is a term 'frequently referred to as a strategy for enabling the process of developing nursing practice' (Simmons, 2004:36) but should be used to support innovation and change for all health and social care. Simmons's (2004) concept analysis of facilitation of practice development highlighted a need for practice developers to reflect critically upon their use of the term facilitation. Rycroft-Malone et al.'s (2004) work associated with the Promoting Action on Research Implementation in Health Services (PARIHS) framework makes inroads into the importance of facilitation within the context of getting evidence into practice which is transferable to practice development. This is achieved by exploring the:

- role of facilitation
- purpose of facilitation
- facilitator role
- skills and attributes of facilitators

a sound tool kit of skills and personal attributes for any practice developer to embrace when supporting innovation and change. Alternatively, Titchen's (2000) 'critical companionship model' offers excellent insight and ways of facilitating learning for individuals and groups in practice. Collectively the works of Simmons (2004), Rycroft-Malone et al. (2004) and Titchen (2000) offer sound insight into the role and purpose of facilitation within the context of practice development. Information on facilitation and practice development can be found in Box 1.3 alongside understanding what facilitation means and involves, and the skills and personal attributes required by a practice developer to support change in practice.

Box 1.3 Facilitation and its importance to practice development

The following publications offer excellent information about what facilitation means and its importance to practice development in supporting innovation and change:

Simmons, M. (2004) 'Facilitation' of practice development: a concept analysis. *Practice Development in Health Care* 3(1): 36–52.

Rycroft-Malone, J. (2004) Research implementation: evidence, context and facilitation – the PARIHS Framework. In: McCormack, B., Manley, K., Garbett, R. *Practice Development in Nursing*. Blackwell Science: Oxford.

Titchen, A. (2000) Professional craft knowledge in patient-centred nursing and the facilitation of its development, University of Oxford DPhil thesis. Ashdale Press: Oxford.

Royal College of Nursing (RCN) Practice Development Facilitation Resources. http://www.rcn.org.uk/resources/practicedevelopment/about-pd/processes/facilitation/

It is imperative to be able to describe a particular activity, that is to say what were you doing, how you did it and what tools and techniques were employed to support the activity. These questions are critical in order to repeat elements that are effective and to share knowledge with others (Simmons, 2004). To this end it is essential that individuals, teams and organisations familiarise themselves with the tools and techniques to facilitate the advancing and evaluating of practice.

Tools and techniques for advancing and evaluating practice

The challenge facing practice developers, nurse consultants/therapists, specialist practitioners and teams in facilitating innovation, change or to evaluate practice(s) is seeking out the various and most appropriate tools and techniques to support the process, and in highlighting how, why and what the effectiveness of the change was. This is important so that others can learn and share from experience and to avoid reinventing the wheel. Prior to beginning and managing the process of change or in developing, implementing and evaluating a new role, innovation or an evaluation of practice ask: Is there anything already available to support you with the project or innovation, change or evaluation? There are many different and diverse individual and organisational assessment tools and techniques to assist in this process as highlighted in Figure 1.6.

It is evident from Figure 1.6 that there are various individual and organisational self-assessment tools and techniques available from the business, marketing and health and social care organisations to aid individuals, teams and organisations with prioritising and developing a strategy for:

1. Assessment tool and technique: Political, Economical, Social and Technological Assessment (PEST analysis)
Brief description: An organisation's operating environment can be analysed by looking at:
• External forces (those factors that an organisation has no control over)
• Internal forces (factors that an organisation has direct control over)

The external environment of an organisation can be analysed by conducting a **PEST** analysis. This is a simple analysis of an organisation's *political, economical, social and technological environment.*
Potential use for practice development: Useful technique to be undertaken when exploring the long-term developments of the of new role, position or service development, redesign or review.
Useful resource details:
Learning Markets. http://www.learnmarketing.net/environment.htm

2. Assessment tool and technique: Strengths, Weaknesses, Opportunities and Threats (SWOT analysis)
Brief description: SWOT analysis is commonly used in marketing as a tool to define plans and set strategies. The SWOT analysis (identification of strengths, weaknesses, opportunities and threats) can help define what needs to be done to adapt to new roles.
Potential use for practice development: Technique to be undertaken at the commencement of a new role or innovation and change as well as periodically throughout the project. The use of development/action plans could be applied to support individual personal/professional development or of the team and the strategic development of the organistion.
Useful resource details: McSherry, R., Pearce, P. (2007) *Clinical Governance: A Guide to Implementation for Health Care Professionals*, 2nd edn. Blackwell Science: Oxford.

3. Assessment tool and technique: Reflective practice
Brief description: Reflective practice described as a 'process of internally examining an issue of concern, triggered by an experience, which creates and clarifies meaning in terms of self and which results in a changed conceptual perspective' (Boyd & Fales 1983). Reflective practice is an ideal way of encouraging individuals, teams and organisations to question and 'confront the social, political [professional] forces which provide the context of their work, and in questioning claims of 'common sense' or 'the way things should be' (Reynolds, 1998:198).
Potential use for practice development: Reflective practice is ideal in supporting practice development because:
• Various models/frameworks generate different approaches for reflective learning to be accessed and applied to different situations and contexts.
• Reflective practice is an essential component of self-awareness and professional practice.
• Reflection in action enables individuals to utilise their current knowledge in support of decision-making.
• Reflection on action enables individuals to define and respond to challenging situations after the event and to evaluate the effectiveness of their action.
• Reflective practice promotes problem-based learning, critical thinking etc.
• There are various strategies to facilitate reflection.

Useful resource details
Boyd, E.M., Fales, A.W. (1983) Reflective learning: key to learning from experience. *Journal of Human Psychology* 23(32): 99–77.

Johns, C. (1999) Reflection as empowerment? *Nursing Inquiry* 6: 241–9.

Kolb, D. A. (1984) *Experiential learning: Experience as the source of learning and development*. Prentice Hall: Englewood Cliffs, NJ.

4. Assessment tool and technique: 'SWAINE' analysis
Brief description: A self-evaluation technique that allows individuals to identify their personal development needs: **S**trengths, **W**eaknesses, **A**spirations, **I**nterests and **N**eeds. Following the self-evaluation an individual action plan can be established for moving forward.
Potential use for practice development: Self-evaluation technique for personal and professional development to support individuals advancing and evaluating practice.
Useful resource details:
Hall, L., Marsh, K. (2000) *Professionalism, Policies and Values: A Reader*. Greenwich University Press: London.

5. Assessment tool and technique: Values Clarification Exercise
Brief description: This is a tool frequently used within practice development (Manley, 1997) for 'developing a common shared vision and purpose. It can be used for developing a common vision about areas as different as development of role definitions, competency, or curriculum frameworks, to, developing strategic direction for different purposes' (RCN, 2002:1).
Potential use for practice development: To clarify and action plan a given innovation and change; to scope and clarify a new role or evaluate an exiting role.
Useful resource details:
Manley, K. (1997) A conceptual framework for advanced practice an action research project operationalizing a advanced practitioner/consultant nurse role. *Journal of Clinical Nursing* 6(3): 179–90.

6. Assessment tool and technique: Force Field Analysis (FFA)
Brief description: A structured group analysis technique that attempts to maximise the success of a proposed solution. When you have agreed on a solution to a problem you may well find the technique useful. Force Field Analysis is a way of identifying the forces and factors in place that support or work against your solution. You may then be able to develop some further ideas to reinforce the driving forces and reduce or eliminate the restraining forces.
Potential use for practice development: To establish/clarify the scope and purpose of a innovation and change; good technique for problem solving.
Useful resource details:
Force Field Analysis, University of Cambridge, Department of Engineering (2004) http://www.mmd.eng.cam.ac.uk/people/ahr/dstools/represent/forcef.htm

7. Assessment tool and technique: Impact Analysis (IA)
Brief description: A tool that can be used to help with problem definition. (It is worth spending an appropriate amount of time making sure that you have defined the problem properly before you set out on an improvement project. No matter how clever we are at coming up with solutions to problems, if we are working on

Figure 1.6 Tools and techniques to support practice development in health and social care. Adapted from the works of Renshaw (2005) in McSherry & Johnson (2005) and the Health Improvement Network (2003)

the wrong problems in the first place we are wasting our time.) It is an excellent way for a team of people to start thinking about a problem and it often serves as an early pointer to possible solutions. Like all of the tools and techniques, it is easy to do but can make a big difference (NHS, 2003).

Potential use for practice development: Excellent technique to use for seeking views and opinions in the early stages 'for getting started' in the role or new innovation and change.

Useful resource details:

The National Health Service – The Improvement Network.
http://www.tin.nhs.uk/sys_upl/templates/StdLeft/StdLeft_disp.asp?pgid=1376&tid=50

8. Assessment tool and technique: Corporate, Management and Clinical Self Assessment Tools

Brief description: The assessment tools provided by the Commission for Health Inspection and Audit (CHIa) known today as the Healthcare Commission (HC) could provide useful tools and templates for establishing the overall systems and processes and standards and quality at an individual, team and organistional level.

Potential use for practice development: These self-assessment tools and techniques could be modified and used to assist you in establishing the initial or base line assessment.

Useful resource details:

Healthcare Commission. http://www.healthcarecommission.org.uk/homepage.cfm

9. Assessment tool and technique: Leadership Qualities Frameworks

Brief description: For self and team assessing.

Potential use for practice development: Ideal for self and team assessing prior to and during innovation and change.

Useful resource details:

National Health Service Leadership Qualities Framework
http://www.nhsleadershipqualities.nhs.uk/

10. Assessment tool and technique: Innovation and Change in Health and Social Care

Brief description: 'The NHS Institute for Innovation and Improvement supports the NHS to transform healthcare for patients and the public by rapidly developing and spreading new ways of working, new technology and world-class leadership (NHS Institute for Innovation and Improvement, 2007); 'to improve the experience of people who use social care by developing and promoting knowledge about good practice in the sector. Using knowledge gathered from diverse sources and a broad range of people and organisations, we develop resources which we share freely, supporting those working in social care and empowering service users' (Social Care Institute for Excellence, 2007).

Potential use for practice development: Both these organisations are ideal resources to access in supporting innovation and change in health and social care.

Useful resource details:

NHS Institute for Innovation and Improvement.
http://www.institute.nhs.uk/organisation/about_nhsi/about_the_nhs_institute.html

SCIE. http://www.scie.org.uk/

Note: This is not an exhaustive list (presented in no particular order) to supporting innovation, change and or evaluation. It is important that you prioritise, establish and employ the tools and techniques most suitable to support the activity.

- getting started in a new role or service
- changing existing practice through review or redesign
- evaluating care.

Self-assessment tools within the context of practice development are about adopting and applying a suitable approach to enable individuals, teams and the organisation to explore the systems that are in place in order to identify strengths and areas for further development (Renshaw, 2005). It is a structured tool asking individuals, teams and the organisation to look at themselves against clearly defined measures, reflect on progress and think about future action, and to help plan and devise a strategy to progress one's role in the future.

The utilisation of these self-assessment frameworks/tools within the context of practice development has the potential to promote effective collaboration by identifying and resolving:

- *Organisational issues*: implementing a new service or reviewing and redesigning existing services
- *Conflicting expectations:* reviewing conflicts of interest between professional groups, teams and individuals
- *Communication issues:* between and within individuals teams and organisations
- *Cultural differences:* between services and departments
- *Resource availability*: for existing or planned service developments.

The benefits of such approaches by extension could be:

- Improved quality
- Enhanced communication
- Shared working
- Complementary standpoints
- Enhanced productivity/outcomes.

McSherry & Johnson (2005)

In order to achieve excellence in health and social care practice it is imperative to understand what we mean by excellence in care and whether or not it is a myth, reality or a continuum attached to expectation.

What do we mean by excellence in care?

The term 'excellence' is being used widely throughout organisations, professionals and businesses as well as health and social care professions. Yet the reality of achieving excellence is fraught with challenge and difficulty; so why do we continue to seek excellence within fields of practice? The pursuit of excellence in health and social care practice according to McSherry (2004) requires:

team-working, interdisciplinary collaboration, effective communication, internal and external partnerships and a willingness to learn and share with and from each other; including users of the NHS (and social care) (2004:140).

To achieve excellence in personal, professional, organisational, managerial, educational, clinical, research and development it is imperative to understand what the term means and how it has been applied in practice. The use of the word 'excellence' or phrase 'excellence in practice' has grown significantly over the past decade. We see excellence, which is undoubtedly increasing in popularity in practice, being advertised and mediated through journalism, business, organisation, management and leadership. Yet the reality of aspiring and achieving this noble goal for every health and social care professional, team and organisation is fraught with difficulty and challenge. This is because despite the importance and use of the word 'excellence' the term is fraught with confusion, misunderstanding and misinterpretation.

Excellence within the context of health and social care

Defining the term 'excellence'

Generally the term excellence is defined by Collins (1987:299) as:

Excel *excellere*, rise to be better or greater than (others)

Excellence the fact or condition of excelling; superiority

Excellency a title of honour applied to various dignitaries

Excellent outstandingly good of its kind.

What the Collins (1987) definition seems to indicate is that excellence is a difficult concept or term to define and articulate for several reasons. Firstly, the term is symbolic with achieving a desired standard or goal which could be individual, team or organisational in nature. Secondly, achieving excellence is indicative of working through a process in order to achieve a desired outcome which again could be individual, team or organisationally orientated. Thirdly, excellence seems to be an outward expression of achieving a status or award which recognises an acquired standard or performance of practice or achievement against a given criterion. Fourthly, excellence is a concept that is associated with outstandingly good performance which is above those of its kind.

By comparing and contrasting the Collins (1987) general definition of excellence with some offered by institutes and departments across health and social care some similarities and differences do emerge. For example the Social Care Institute for Excellence (SCIE) associate excellence with improving the experience of people who use social care services, by ensuring that knowledge about what works is readily accessible. We pull together knowledge from diverse sources through working with a broad range of organisations and people. We share this knowledge freely, supporting those working in social care and empowering service users.

Similarly the Department of Health (DH, formerly DoH) link excellence to the clinical governance framework defined as

a framework through which NHS organisations are accountable for continuously improving the quality of their services and safeguarding high standards of care by creating an environment in which excellence in clinical care will flourish (1998a).

Taking the Collins (1987), SCIE and DH definitions and interpretations of excellence into account it is evident that several key themes emerge about what excellence is and is not.

Firstly, excellence is an outward expression of an achievement of a desired outcome against a set of criteria which is above the given or expected standard of practice. Secondly, excellence is a very nebulous concept making it difficult to define because it is associated with individuals', teams' and organisations' visions, goals and aspirations which could change and shift with acquired experience, knowledge, and education and training. Thirdly, achieving excellence in practice is challenging and difficult because it is hard to isolate and differentiate what it is that makes an individual, team or organisation stand out from others based on a given set of criteria, standards and frameworks. Fourthly, excellence is associated with having robust frameworks, systems and processes in place for the gathering and presentation of evidence against a given set of criteria. Finally, given the fact that there are so many different accreditation bodies describing what excellence in health and social care is and is not makes it both challenging and rewarding for individuals, teams and organisations to work with and across the various systems and processes in order to demonstrate an acquired standard of practice. It is without doubt that excellence is and will remain a difficult concept to define and recognise in health and social care. However, as Moullin (2002:1) suggests, the 'vast majority of people working in health and social care are concerned with the quality of the service they provide, indicating that the strive for quality and excellence are interchangeable and may vary depending on the perceptions, experiences and attitudes and behaviours of people notwithstanding the systems and processes required to gather and present the evidence against a set of standards or performance indicators. The challenge for health and social care is in developing, implementing and evaluating the systems and processes to denote an acquired level of excellence.

Achieving excellence (the process) for oneself, team and organisation

The challenge facing individual health and social care professionals, teams and organisations is how to start advancing or evaluating practice in a busy, stressful and time-conscious environment like those of the health and social care environments of today. The key to resolving these and other obstacles is to 'recognise the complexity of the practice environment if they want to effect change and tailor any developments to suit the local context' (Page, 2001).

Despite the proliferation of information highlighting the value of practice development to encourage lifelong learning and professional development, minimal research as suggested by McCormack et al. (2006) has been undertaken to demonstrate the overall impact practice development has had on improving the outcomes within the practice setting. The challenge and difficulties facing individuals, teams and organisations is in selecting a suitable organisational framework or accreditation framework that illustrates the efficiency and effectiveness of their practice(s) or service(s).

Case study 1.1 Facilitating and accrediting excellence in practice: the opportunities and challenges surrounding accreditation

A specialist learning disabilities residential home caring for six clients with a diverse range of needs sought to demonstrate that the service and care they provided to their users and local public was of the highest quality and standard of practice.

The challenge facing the team was in selecting an appropriate accreditation scheme that could both facilitate and accredit the service.

The information in this section is designed to illustrate how organisational accreditation and practice development may support a team such as the one above in responding to the challenges and difficulties associated with demonstrating excellence in practice.

Organisational accreditation and practice development

Over the past 15 years the development of organisational standards and the measurement of practice have emerged as challenges for teams and organisations in demonstrating best practice against a rigorous set of criteria or standards. Different organisations have developed schemes that help practice areas to measure the quality of the service they provide. The Royal College of Nursing Dynamic Standard Setting System (Kitson, 1994) was one such measurement tool. Total Quality Management and the Qualpac system were favoured by management in the early 1990s. Today different bodies measure different aspects of service provision such as the Investors in People scheme (IiP Scheme), which measures how good the organisation is in supporting its staff. More recent initiatives include Nursing Development Unit and Practice Development Unit accreditation schemes (Lathan & Vaughan, 1997).

Initially Nursing Development Units (NDUs) were seen as one way in which excellent practice could be developed by practitioners and showcased to the wider nursing body. NDUs were units that were given financial support, initially by the King's Fund, to develop and extend nursing practice. One of the earliest units was at the Burford Unit, in Oxford, where practitioners provided holistic patient-centred care to elderly patients in one particular unit. The notion of NDUs has grown and in the Durham and Tees Valley area NDUs were verified by a local nursing forum. The development of new and innovative practice is encouraged and units are measured against a set of criteria based on clinical nursing practice.

Practice development units emerged based on schemes similar to NDUs but having a multi-professional approach rather than focusing on nursing care. To gain the status of a Practice Development Unit wards or departments had to demonstrate to external assessors their application of multi-professional practice in their area. This was measured against set criteria that had been developed by the awarding body. Local universities developed Practice Development Centres that would accredit departments using their set criteria. To gain external validation of practice was seen by some to be a useful tool in developing their practice. One fundamental drawback to this system was in the maintenance of best practice once the accreditation had taken place.

Within health and social care many other organisational standards and accreditation frameworks have emerged to assist health and social care professionals in demonstrating an achieved level of quality for a given service(s), for example:

- The Healthcare Commission (HC)
- European Foundation Quality Management (EFQM)
- Investors in People (IiP)
- Clinical Negligence Scheme for Trust (CNST) and Litigation Health Authority
- Charter Mark
- Social Care Institute for Excellence (SCIE).

The potential benefit of each of these frameworks is in offering a set of criteria for measuring a given practice to a set standard or level of excellence. For example, IiP relates to assessing organisational support for staff and staff development. HC and SCIE review how health and social care organisations are meeting the challenge of implementing clinical governance. Both of these examples are different, but yet equally valuable in advancing and evaluating practice.

The disadvantages of organisational standards and accreditation within health and social care today is in the duplication of time, resources and support needed for individuals, teams and organisations in collecting, collating and providing the evidence to demonstrate the standard(s). Health and social care organisations seem to be pressurised not just for meeting the criteria for one award but several at any one time. Organisational standards and accreditation schemes are essential for demonstrating acquired levels of excellence within any organisation. They provide excellent frameworks for promoting quality improvements and as a result support practice development, making practices open and accountable. Organisational standard measurement is an integral part of any quality improvement and therefore an integral part of developing practice. Practice areas need to provide evidence to the accrediting bodies to show how they have achieved a particular standard. To put all of these standards into practice and to develop a framework that demonstrates to each awarding body the achievement of the standard is time-consuming and confusing to many health and social care professionals. Yet despite the upsurge in organisational schemes and associated standards many health and social care professionals struggle to understand and appreciate the potential value of these schemes in promoting excellence in practice (McSherry et al., 2003).

Potential value of seeking excellence in practice on future health and social care practices

Excellence in practice is about promoting and developing practice that creates a working organisational culture that

> acts in partnership, providing support between clinical practice, education and management, enabling them to increase research utilisation' [and the practising of evidence-based care] (Bassett, 1996:918).

Based on the critique of the excellence-based terms and phrases it would appear that 'excellence in practice' provides a foundation for individuals, teams and organisations to use in the quest for quality. This is because the phrase 'excellence in practice' encapsulates the principles of evidence-based practice within the clinical governance agenda because excellence is about minimising risks through the development of a learning organisation (Stanton, 2007). Excellence in practice is about encouraging and facilitating the development of best practice based on ensuring effective communication, collaboration and team building. Furthermore, excellence in practice should form part of everyone's role and responsibility as part of their job description, contract of employment and professional code of practice. Finally, excellence in practice according to McSherry (2004) is interdependent on the unification of several important aspects of an organisation's systems and processes that denote excellence as outlined in Figure 1.7.

- Working in organisations
- Collaborative working
- User-focused care
- Continuous quality improvements
- Performance management
- Measuring efficiency and effectiveness

Figure 1.7 Key factors for achieving excellence in practice

Working in organisations

Working in organisations is about exploring the initiatives under the policy outlined in *Improving Working Lives* (DH, 2006b) and concentrates on team development, communication and the sharing of information. It is about working towards creating a working environment and culture upon which excellence can flourish (McCormack et al., 2002).

Collaborative working

Collaborative working focuses on multi-professional working and development as the main issue for achievement of quality improvement.

User-focused care

The main theme of the modernisation and reforming agenda is about encouraging user participation and representation so that users' views and feedback are both directly and indirectly incorporated into the development of practice. This theme focuses on the standards to be reached to achieve this in practice.

Continuous quality improvements

Within all quality improvement systems that have been introduced into the health service over the past 12 years the inclusion of improving the quality of care has always been an issue. Can the individual and the team incorporate the concept of quality issues in everything that they do? This standard aims to make quality part of everyday working practice.

Performance management

To manage effectively is to improve performance and user satisfaction. This key component should concentrate on how this can be achieved in practice.

Measuring efficiency and effectiveness

To demonstrate efficiency and effectiveness in practice is to show how the systems can be measured and audited to illustrate developments and improvements in practice.

Having identified the key factors that appear to denote the degree of excellence in practice it is imperative to highlight ways of making this happen in reality.

Achieving excellence in practice

Several important factors appear to be essential for achieving excellence in practice. Ensure you have a sound vision and philosophy for the organisation that transcends through the various departments and teams to the individual. To facilitate this process the use of one of the various models/ frameworks/schemes described previously is ideal in promoting best practice within the context of clinical governance. This is because the use of a model/ framework/scheme focuses attention on achieving the vision by strategically focusing the goals to become pertinent to all health and social care professionals, teams and organisations and builds upon current practice developments. The scoring framework for many of the excellence in practice frameworks supports the notion that benchmarking is viewed as a process of seeking, finding, implementing and sustaining best practice. It is a continuous process of measuring services and practices against set criteria that demonstrate best practice. The use of excellence in practice frameworks provides a useful method and approach in demonstrating the contribution practice development makes to teams and organisations by adopting a proactive style to measuring and evaluating new or existing practices (McSherry and Bassett, 2002). In this instance benchmarking provides an opportunistic structured approach to promoting best practice by encouraging health and social care professionals, teams and organisations to share and network via an identified area of care. A benchmark is the desired standard or level of performance an individual, team or organisation is aspiring to emulate.

Different methods of benchmarking can be undertaken, dependent upon the practice under review. For example:

- Internally, by comparing similar processes but within different sections of the organisation, for example, patient waiting times in different parts of outpatients.
- Externally, through competitive benchmarking, used to compare similar size organisations' performance against certain standards such as the cost of treatments or interventions.
- Functional benchmarking, the isolation of functional processes and comparison of the findings, such as non-attendance for outpatients' appointments.

Benchmarking within the Excellence in Practice Accreditation Scheme (EPAS) (McSherry et al., 2003) uses a combination of benchmarks to assess the level or standard of practice. To quantify this a rating, based on each benchmark, is awarded. The ratings are then processed to enable an overall score to be awarded to the team or organisation. The level scored is then used to identify good practice for dissemination or where a team or organisation needs to develop the practice to improve the quality of provision. This is an effective way of demonstrating evidence-based practice within the context of clinical governance as the star awarding system is recognised throughout quality enhancement schemes.

Conclusions

By focusing on what practice development is and is not, it is possible to illustrate how individuals, teams and organisations could embrace the underpinning philosophies, principles, purposes, methodologies, tools and techniques to promote and demonstrate excellence in health and social care practice. Excellence is an ever-changing term and a very nebulous concept to define and articulate making it perhaps never achievable because it is always changing as practice and practices changes as a direct and indirect consequence of change itself. Furthermore, organisations, teams and individual aspirations and motivation change as a part of personal and professional experience, which again shifts goals and vision and the way we regard the term 'excellence'. What is emerging is the fact that excellence in health and social care practice can be enhanced or inhibited by focusing attention on the hidden ingredients contained in practice development and by exploring the following core themes:

- Working in organisations
- Collaborative working
- User-focused care
- Continuous quality improvement
- Performance management (integrated governance)
- Measuring efficiency and effectiveness.

The emphasis of the series of books will be based on demonstrating how and why these core themes are applied to reveal a framework for promoting excellence in practice.

Key points

- To address and respond to the growing pressures to change, reform or modernise, it is important that health and social care professionals recognise what, why and how practice development may aid the pursuit of excellence in practice.
- Despite the potential benefits of practice development in promoting excellence it is imperative that individuals, teams and organisations understand what the term means.
- Ultimately the purpose of practice development is about ensuring that person/ patient centredness is at the heart of all innovation and change.
- Practice development is about enabling health and social care workers, teams and organisations to transform the culture and context in which care is provided. In order to achieve this it is about developing partnerships, providing support between clinical practice, education and management, enabling them to increase research utilisation.
- Facilitation is undoubtedly an important factor for effective practice development and is an essential concept to understand in relation to supporting innovation and change.
- Self-assessment tools within the context of practice development are about adopting and applying a suitable approach to enable individuals, teams and the organisation to explore the systems that are in place in order to identify strengths and areas for further development.

- Excellence is an ever-changing term and a very nebulous concept to define and articulate making it perhaps never achievable because it is always changing as practice and practices changes as a direct and indirect consequence of change itself.
- Excellence in practice should form part of everyone's role and responsibility as part of their job description, contract of employment and professional code of practice.

 Activity 1.2 Feedback

The terms practice development and excellence in health and social care practice are difficult and challenging to define and operationalise on a daily basis. Practice development offers a new, dynamic and creative way of promoting excellence in practice through collaboration, team working, communication and by involving the users and providers of care. Practice development is a way to achieving excellence by encouraging people to embrace innovation and change at an individual, team and organisational level.

Further reading

McCormack, B., Manley, K., Garbett, R. (2004) *Practice Development in Nursing.* Blackwell Publishing: Oxford.

McSherry, R., Bassett, C. (eds) (2002) *Practice Development in the Clinical Setting: A Guide to Implementation.* Nelson Thornes: Cheltenham.

Useful links

Developing Practice Subscribers Area. Foundation of Nursing Studies: London. www.fons.org/dp/

Royal College of Nursing (RCN) Practice Development Facilitation Resources. http://www.rcn.org.uk/resources/practicedevelopment/about-pd/processes/facilitation/

References

Bassett, C. (1996) The sky's the limit. *Nursing Standard* 10(25): 16–19.

Burke, D.E., Culligan, C.J., Holt, L.E., McKinnon, W.C. (2000) Equipment designed to stimulate proprioceptive neuro-muscular facilitation flexibility training. *Journal of Strength and Conditioning Research* 14: 135–9.

Cambron, B., Cain, L. (2004) Practice development: what we can learn from our British partners. *Creative Nursing* 10(2): 14–15.

Clarke, C.L., Wilcockson, J. (2001) Professional and organizational learning: analysing the relationship with the development of practice. *Journal of Advanced Nursing* 34(2): 264–72.

Collins, W. (1987) *Collins Universal English Dictionary.* Readers Union Ltd: Glasgow.

Cross, K.D. (1996) An analysis of the concept facilitation. *Nurse Education Today* 16: 350–5.

Developing Practice Network (2002) Foundation of Nursing Studies: London. www.dpnetwork.org.uk

Elwyn, G.J. (1998) Professional and practice development plans for primary care teams: Life after the postgraduate education allowance. *British Medical Journal* 316: 1619–20.

Garbett, R., McCormack, B. (2001) The experience of practice development: an exploratory telephone interview study. *Journal of Clinical Nursing* 10(1): 94–2001.

Garbett, R., McCormack, B. (2002) A concept analysis of practice development. *Nursing Times Research* 7(2): 87–100.

Glover, D. (1998) The art of practice development. *Nursing Times* 94(36): 58–9.

Glover, D. (2002) What is practice development? In: McSherry, R., Bassett, C. (eds) *Practice Development in the Clinical Setting: A Guide to Implementation.* Nelson Thornes: Cheltenham.

Gustafsson, C., Fargerberg, I. (2004) Reflection: the way to professional development. *Journal of Clinical Nursing* 13(3): 271–80.

Haag-Heitman, B., Kramer, A. (1998) Creating a clinical practice development model. *American Journal of Nursing* 8: 39–43.

Habermas, J. (1972) *Knowledge and Human Interests; Theory and Practice; Communication and the Evolution of Society* (translated by J. J. Shapiro). London: Heinemann.

Health Improvement Network (2003) *The Improvement Network.* NHS, East Midlands. http://www.tin.nhs.uk/index.asp?pgid=1155 (accessed 21 November 2007).

Health Service Executive Southern Ireland (2007) *A Strategy for Practice Development.* HSE, Nursing and Midwifery Planning Development Unit: Dublin.

Hunter, D., Bailey, A., Taylor, B. (1996) *The Facilitation of Groups.* Gower: Basingstoke.

Hynes, G. (2004) Exploring philosophical underpinnings for practice development education in Ireland. Paper presented at the 5th Annual International Research Conference. School of Nursing and Midwifery Studies, University of Dublin, Trinity College, Dublin, November.

Kitson, A. (1994) *Clinical Nursing Practice Development and Research Activity in the Oxford Region.* Centre for Practice Development and Research, National Institute for Nursing: Oxford.

Kitson, A.L., Ahmed, L.B., Harvey, G., Seers, K., Thompson, D. (1996) From research to practice: one organisational model for promoting research-based practice. *Journal of Advanced Nursing* 23(3): 430–40.

Lathan, J., Vaughan, B. (1997) *Directory of NDU Activities.* King's Fund: London.

Manley, K. (1997) Practice development: a growing and significant movement. *Nursing in Critical Care* 2(1): 5.

Manley, K., McCormack, B. (2003) Practice development: purpose, methodology, facilitation and evaluation. *Nursing in Critical Care* 8(1): 22–9.

McCormack, B., Garbett, R. (2003) The characteristics, qualities and skills of practice developers. *Journal of Clinical Nursing* 12(3): 317–25.

McCormack, B., Manley, K., Kitson, A., Titchen, A., Harvey, G. (1999) Towards practice development – a vision in reality or reality without vision. *Journal of Nursing Management* 7(5): 255–64.

McCormack, B., Kitson, A., Harvey, G., Rycroft-Malone, J., Titchen, A., Seers, K. (2002) Getting evidence into practice: the meaning of 'context'. *Journal of Advanced Nursing* 38(1): 94–104.

McCormack, B., Manley, K., Garbett, R. (2004) *Practice Development in Nursing.* Blackwell Publishing: Oxford.

McCormack, B., Dewar, B., Wright, J., Garbett, R., Harvey, G., Ballantine, K. (2006) *A Realist Synthesis of Evidence Relating to Practice Development: Executive Summary.* NHS Quality Improvement Scotland and NHS Education for Scotland: Edinburgh.

McSherry, R. (1999) Achieving quality improvements. *Health Care Risk Report* 5(7): 14–15.

McSherry, R. (2004) Practice development and health care governance: a recipe for modernisation. *Journal of Nursing Management* 12: 137–46.

McSherry, R., Bassett, C. (eds) (2002) *Practice Development in the Clinical Setting: A Guide to Implementation*. Nelson Thornes: Cheltenham.

McSherry, R., Driscoll, J. (2004) Practice development: promoting quality improvement in orthopaedic care . . . as well as one's self. *Journal of Orthopaedic Nursing* 8(3): 171–8.

McSherry, R., Johnson, S. (2005) (eds) *Demystifying the Nurse/Therapist Consultant: A Foundation Text*. Nelson Thornes: Cheltenham.

McSherry, R., Pearce, P. (2007) *Clinical Governance. A Guide to Implementation for Healthcare Professionals*, 2nd edn. Blackwell Publishing: Oxford.

McSherry, R., Warr, J. (2006) Practice development: Confirming the existence of a knowledge and evidence base. *Practice Development in Health Care* 5(2): 55–79.

McSherry, R., Kell, J., Mudd, D. (2003) Practice development: best practice using Excellence in Practice Accreditation Scheme. *British Journal of Nursing* 12(10): 623–9.

Mooney, M., Nolan, L. (2006) A critique of Freies's perspectives on critical social theory in nursing education. *Nurse Education Today* 26: 240–4.

Moullin, M. (2002) *Delivering Excellence in Health and Social Care: Quality, Excellence and Performance Measurement*. Open University Press: Buckingham.

O'Neal, H., Manley, K. (2007) Action planning: making your changes happen in clinical practice. *Nursing Standard* 21(35): 35–41.

Page, S. (2001) Demystifying practice development. *Nursing Times* 97(22): 36–7.

Page, S., Hamer, S. (2002) Practice development – time to realize the potential. *Practice Development in Health Care* 1(1): 2–17.

Page, S., Allsopp, D., Casley, S. (1998) *The Practice Development Unit*. Whurr Publishing: London.

Pickering, S., Thompson, J. (2003) *Clinical Governance and Best Value: Meeting the Modernisation Agenda*. Churchill Livingstone: London.

Pitkanen, A., Kuronen, M., Pukuri, T., Valimakii, M. (2004) Practice development. Developing nurses' capabilities to deputize for ward sisters. *Journal of Psychiatric and Mental Health Nursing* 11(2): 253–9.

Renshaw, T. (2005) Getting started as a nurse/therapist consultant. In: McSherry, R., Johnson, S. (2005) (eds) *Demystifying the Nurse/Therapist Consultant: A Foundation Text*. Nelson Thornes: Cheltenham.

Reynolds, M. (1998) Reflection and critical reflection in management learning. *Management Learning* 29(2): 183–200.

Royal College of Nursing (RCN) (2003) *Values Clarification: A Tool For Developing A Common Vision and Strategic Direction*. RCN: London. http://www.did.stu.mmu.ac.ul/carn/studydays/values%20clarification%20v3.do (accessed 21 November 2007).

Rycroft-Malone, J., Seers, K., Titchen, A., Harvey, G.B., Kitson, A., McCormack, B. (2004) What counts as evidence in evidence-based practice? *Journal of Advanced Nursing* 47(10): 81–90.

Simmons, M. (2004) Facilitation of practice development: a concept analysis *Practice Development in Health Care* 3(1): 36–52.

Social Care Institute for Excellence (SCIE) (2007) *Practice Guide 09. Dignity in Care*. SCIE: London. http://www.scie.org.uk/publication/practiceguides/practiceguide09/index.asp (accessed 21 November 2007).

Soltis-Jarrett, V. (1997) The facilitator in participatory action research. Le raison d'être. *Advances in Nursing* 20: 45–54.

Stanton, A.P. (2007) Forward. In: McSherry, R., Pearce, P. (2007) *Clinical Governance: A Guide to Implementation for Healthcare Professionals*, 2nd edn. Blackwell Publishing: Oxford.

Taylor, R., Coombes, L., Bartlett, H. (2002) The impact of a practice development project on the quality of in-patient small group therapy. *Health Services Management Research* 16(1): 1–12.

Walker, K. (2003) Practice development in a postmodern world. *Collegian 2003* 10(3): 17–21.

Walsh, K., McCallister, M., Morgan, A., Thornhill, J. (2004) Motivating change: using motivational interviewing in practice development. *Practice Development in Health Care* 3(2): 92–100.

Wong, F.K. (2002) Development of advanced nursing practice in Hong Kong: a celebration of ten years work. *Hong Kong Nursing Journal* 38(3): 25–9.

Yacopeth, N. (2007) *Consolidating Theory, Research and Practice: Exploring Critical Social Theory*. Sydney, Australia. http://www.clinfohealth.nsw.gov.au/hospic/stvincents/2000/CONSOLIDATING%20THEORYhtm (accessed 22 November 2007).

2 The drivers for excellence in health and social care

Introduction

This chapter is adapted from the works of McSherry & Pearce (2007) on clinical governance and is reproduced with kind permission from Blackwell Science. The chapter identifies the key drivers for excellence in health and social care, which, we believe, can be distilled and categorised into three main categories: political, professional and public demands. Within these three categories it is evident that working toward achieving excellence in health and social care practice at either an individual, team and organisational level is about continuing to improve the quality of care that the public should rightfully expect in a modern society (McSherry, 2004).

Background

No single factor has lead to the government's current position for modernisation, improvement or system reform of health and social care services in the quest for excellence in practice. We argue that patients' and carers' expectations and demands of all health and social care professionals have significantly increased over the past decade. In the 1980s and early 1990s public awareness of health and social care provision was increased through target facilitation by the publication of significant documents, notably *The Patients' Charter* (1992) and *The Citizens' Charter* (1993) both of which were readily and freely made available to the public. These charters may have, on the one hand, increased patients' and carers' expectations of health and social care, by offering information about certain rights to care. On the other hand, the responsibilities of the patients to use these rights in a responsible way has been overused, resulting in higher demands for care and services in an already busy organisation. From the 1990s to 2005 we have seen a huge emphasis placed on patient and public involvement (PPI) in the planning, delivery and quality assessment of care. Public and patient involvement has been targeted at both a national and local level both directly and indirectly through the establishment of Patient Advice and Liaison Services (DH, 2000a) within every NHS organisation. Nationally we have witnessed the establishment of the Commission for Patient and Public Involvement (DH, 2003) resulting in the creation of Patient and Public User Involvement Fora. Similarly the development of the Over View and Scrutiny Committees for Health (HMSO, 2002) has the sole purpose of seeking and representing public opinion on the quality of health and social care.

Activity 2.1 Contributing factors driving for excellence in health and social care practice

Write down what you feel are the contributing factors driving for excellence in health and social care practice.

Read on and compare your findings in the Activity Feedback at the end of the chapter.

Contributing factors such as changes in health and social care policy, demographic changes, increased patient dependency, changes in healthcare delivery systems, trends towards greater access to health and social care information, advances in health technology, increased media coverage of healthcare and rising numbers of complaints going to litigation have influenced the need for a unified approach to providing and assuring clinical quality via clinical governance (McNeil, 1998). These will now be debated in further detail under three broad headings and associated subheadings (Figure 2.1).

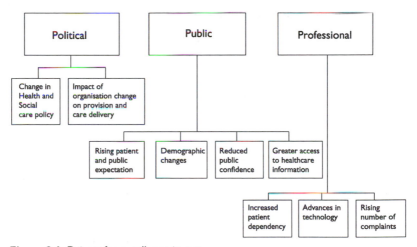

Figure 2.1 Drivers for excellence in care

Political

Political drivers for excellence in practice should be viewed with both a capital and small 'p'. The capital 'P' refers to those drivers resulting directly from government and policy. The small 'p' relates to organisation and personal factors that influence change and policy decision-making at a local level. A view held by Jarrold (2005):

politics with a small p makes the world go round. Getting things done, seeking support, building alliances, compromising – that's all politics, and inescapable and natural (2005:35).

The challenge for healthcare professionals is translating policy into practice and keeping up-to-date with changes in health care policy.

Changes in health and social care policy

In brief, the NHS was established in 1948 following the passing of the National Health Services Act 1946 which committed the government at the time to financially fund health and social care services 'which rested on the principles of collectivism, comprehensiveness, equality and universality' (Allsop, 1986:12). The politicians at the time thought that addressing the health and social care needs of the public would subsequently reduce the amount of money required to maintain health and social care. The assumption was that disease could be controlled. However, this was not the case. Health and social care activity spiralled resulting in uncontrollable year on year expenditures to meet the rise in public demand for healthcare. In an attempt to manage this trend, the government introduced the principles of general management into the NHS Griffiths Report (1983). The philosophy of general management was concerned with developing efficiency and effectiveness of services. The rationale behind this report was to provide services that addressed healthcare needs (effectiveness) within optimal resource allocation (efficiency).

The report recommended that 'general managers should be appointed at all levels in the NHS to provide leadership, introduce a continual search for change and cost improvement, motivate staff and develop a more dynamic management approach' (Ham, 1986:33).

Key organisational processes were identified as missing in the report.

Absence of this general management support means that there is no driving force seeking and accepting direct and personal responsibility for developing management plans, securing their implementation and monitoring actual achievement. It means that the process of devolution of responsibility, including discharging responsibility to units, is far too slow' (Griffiths, 1983:12).

This approach, whilst noble at the time, was concerned with organisational, managerial and financial aspects of the NHS, to the detriment of other important issues such as clinical quality. This style of management further evolved with the introduction of the White Paper *Working for Patients* (1989), culminating in the development of a 'market forces' approach to the organisation and delivery of the healthcare services by the creation of a purchaser and provider spilt. Health authorities and general practitioner fundholders were allocated resources (finances) to purchase care for their local population at the best price. It appears that the purchaser/provider split 'did nothing more than engender a lack of strategic co-ordination between healthcare agencies, as they were encouraged to meet their own financial agendas rather than work in partnership' (Wilkinson & Miers, 1999:86) or in the maintenance and development of clinical quality. These imbalances led to the introduction of the White Papers *The New NHS Modern and Dependable* (DH, 1997), *Quality in the NHS* (DH, 1998a), *Every Child Matters* (DH, 2005), *Our Health, Our Care, Our Say* (DH, 2006) and *Options for Excellence* (DH, 2006) putting quality on a par with organisational, managerial and financial aspects of health and social care via what is arguably 'clinical governance'. A framework 'which is viewed positively by many healthcare professionals as an ambitious shift of focus by the current government in moving away from finance to quality' (McSherry & Haddock, 1999:114).

This approach to providing health and social care services places a statutory duty to match moral responsibilities and harmonises managers' and clinicians' responsibilities/duties more closely in assuring clinical and non-clinical quality. The impact of these reforms (DoH, 1989; 1997; 1998a) has enhanced public awareness and expectations of care placing a strong emphasis on achieving quality through restructuring and changing of services.

Taking into account the many recent policy changes within health and social care a way forward to achieving excellence in care, as advocated in *Options for Excellence* (DH, 2006) is by manifesting a vision through encouraging participation, partnership building and working in order to change perceptions of staff and public in order to achieve a state of professionalism. The vision is that by 2020

> we will have a highly skilled, valued and accountable workforce drawn from all sections of the community. This trained and trusted workforce will work within the 'social model of care', looking at individuals in their personal, family and community context, and providing imaginative and innovative services. Alongside carers, volunteers and workers from a range of other services, the workforce will make a positive difference, contributing to people's health, happiness and well-being (DH, 2006:6).

The social model is based on achieving the following:

> The 'social model' looks at individuals in their personal, family and community context, bringing their strengths, capabilities and resources to bear on their own situations and the barriers to the outcomes they want. It looks at the local support networks as well as the publicly-funded services to help them to stay independent, in control and engaged with the wider community. The model supports earlier interventions that can focus on extra support to reinforce individual and family coping strategies (DH, 2006:75).

The social model is an ideal for achieving excellence in care because it transcends professional disciplines focusing on stakeholder networking from the diverse range of services and individuals who come in contact with adults and children. The emphasis is placed on multi-disciplinary and shared working relationships which continue to keep the person at the centre of care.

The impact of organisational change on the provision of care delivery

With the increases in the numbers of patients admitted with multiple needs, health and social care organisations have had to change the pattern of care delivery in order to accommodate this growing need, leading to the development of: acute medical and surgical assessment units, preoperative assessment units, multiple needs and rehabilitation units, acute mental health assessment units. Latterly we have witnessed a rise in the development of services dedicated to maintain individuals in the community. Initiatives such as Mental Health Crisis Intervention Teams (DH, 2001) and the management of patients with long-term conditions such as diabetes and chronic obstructive pulmonary disease. This style of service provision is about maximising the use of acute and community beds by encouraging collaborative working between primary and secondary and social care in the management and maintenance of the patient in the most appropriate setting. For example, in the shared care approach to the management of patients who have diabetes, the care is shared between the GP and consultant endocrinologist with the backing of the diabetic team (diabetes nurse specialist, dietician, podiatrist, ophthalmologist and pharmacist, care manager etc.). Initiatives such as hospital at home schemes (where possible, maintaining the patient in their own home) are beginning to be developed along with public and private sector partnerships (acute illness managed in hospital, rehabilitation continued in private nursing home until ready for discharge).

The driving force behind these innovations could be attributed to the reduction in junior doctors' hours (DH, 1998b) and the possible effects of the European Working Time Directive (DH, 2004), culminating in the development of nurse practitioners particularly in highly busy areas such as acute medical admissions and accident and emergency departments, a concept reinforced recently by the introduction of nurse consultants and therapists (McSherry & Johnson, 2005) to accommodate the increasing demands for health and social care due to the growing life expectancy with people with greater health care needs. These changes to health and social care delivery are directed towards enhancing the quality of care and in raising public confidence.

Public

The public has contributed significantly towards the pursuit of excellence in practice through direct and indirect ways. These vary in nature from rising expectation to changes in demography.

Rising patient and public expectations and involvement

The Patients' Charter (1992) *Raising the Standards* was distributed to all householders in the UK detailing patients' and carers' rights to healthcare. The main principles behind this charter were that of informing and empowering the patients. This charter led to patients being viewed as consumers of healthcare. As consumers they are entitled to certain rights and standards of care. These standards included the right to be registered with a general practitioner, to have a named consultant and qualified nurse as an inpatient, along with the right to be seen within 30 minutes of any specified appointment time with a healthcare practitioner. Similarly within social care it is about having more choice in the care received in a care or residential care home or about having access to housing, social security etc. The Patients' Charter reinforced the aims of the Citizens' Charter (1993) by empowering the individual to become actively involved in the delivery of health services by the granting of certain rights. This style of care delivery was unique, as, previously, patients tended to be seen as passive recipients of often paternalistic methods (the 'doctor knows best') of providing care. The benefit of these charters have been variable: some individuals (public and health and social care professionals) are unaware of their existence in promoting raised standards. Alternatively, many patients/carers are much more aware and informed of certain rights to treatments and healthcare interventions. In general, the majority of health and social care professionals have taken up and accepted the challenges posed by these charters in improving the delivery and organisation of care. This may be evidenced by reviewing waiting time results and league tables for given services. It could be argued that the Patients' Charter has led to a more questioning public about their rights and expectations of care, such as: What is the problem? How will the condition be treated? What are the alternatives? What are the potential risks and benefits of all treatment options? These are genuine concerns for the public that need addressing.

A limitation of the Patients' Charter was raising rights and expectations to care services, which at times are difficult to achieve for many caring organisations. For example, to have a named care manager or nurse assess, plan, implement and evaluate care needs from admission to discharge or throughout the social care setting was impractical and overestimated. Similarly it is difficult for all outpatient attendees to be seen by their consultant on every visit. The consequence of raising expectations, which are not achievable, results in dissatisfaction with services and a higher incidence of complaints. The principles behind the charters are plausible providing the services are resourced sufficiently. Furthermore the publication of the Patients' Charter's waiting times and league tables have highlighted inequalities in the provision of healthcare by demonstrating good and poor performers of services. For example, access to services for day case surgery could be variable according to region or demographic status of the local population and geography. League tables alone do not provide the public with the background information of the local community health trends or the availability of healthcare services for individual trusts, hence the disparity of service provision between trusts. It could be the case that it may be inappropriate to perform day case surgery for hernia repairs in a hospital situated in a rural area with a large elderly population because of accessibility of services and appropriateness of the surgery to the patients' needs. This is more evident in society today with an ever increasing elderly population with complex physical, social and psychological needs placing yet further demands on the health service, making the Patients' Charter standards more difficult to achieve.

The strive towards excellence in practice has occurred through the White Paper (DH, 1997); we have seen a dramatic shift from limited patient and public involvement to an almost statutory requirement. This is evident by the publication of the Freedom of Information Act (DH, 2000c) and the Patient and Public Fora (DH, 2003). These Acts and policy changes encourage NHS organisations to systematically involve patients and users in making decisions about the development, provision and experience of the services they have accessed. The Patient and Public Fora (DH, 2003) and Patient Advisory Liaison Services (PALS) are two national examples of the government's commitment to improving services for the patients and the public. A key outcome of the government's health polices is placing the patients at the heart of service development, delivery and evaluation. PPI is critical in a modern consumerist society in ensuring that services are truly representative and reflective of patient and public needs. This is important in light of changes in demography and dependency.

Demographic changes

Public health policy and findings from national surveys reiterate the government's publication of *The Health of the Nation* (DH, 1991), which highlighted that life expectancy (National Statistics, 2004) will increase for all, along with changes in the patterns of mortality and morbidity, for example, increased prevalence of diabetes and obesity (Press Association, 2005). As a consequence of these demographic changes together with changes in morbidity patterns, the NHS needs to provide more acute, continuing care and primary care services for an increasing elderly population and the changes in patterns of disease and illness associated with societal change. To reduce health and social care demands, *The Health of the Nation* document set targets for reducing morbidity (disease and disability trends) by concentrating upon health promotion and disease prevention; for example, the reduction of strokes by the active management of high blood pressure (hypertension) and the reduction of deaths attributed to coronary heart disease by promoting healthy eating, exercise and where necessary the prescription of statins (cholesterol lowering drugs) (DH, 2000b). The general population changes indicate there has been and will continue to be a large increase in the numbers of people living to and beyond 65, 75 and 85. Longevity seems to be on the increase for all (DH, 1991), reinforcing the growing trends of high dependency patients. Longevity is not the only demographic challenge facing the future NHS; we have seen widening inequalities in health, wealth and disease. There are growing public health concerns around obesity, sexual health, drug and alcohol related problems, all of which will lead to greater demands on the health service and its employees.

Lack of public confidence in care provision due to media coverage of poor clinical practices

The media continues to play a major role in increasing patients' and carers' awareness of the NHS through the publication of clinical successes and failures in the organisations, such as the Bristol case (Royal Bristol Infirmary Inquiry, 2001) and the Shipman Inquiry (2005). The Bristol case relates to consultant paediatric cardiac surgeons who were found to have a death rate for paediatric heart surgery significantly higher than the national average. This only became known as result of whistle blowing (*Lancet*, 1998). The Shipman case involved a general practitioner in Hyde, Manchester, who was found to have murdered hundreds of his patients mainly by an overdose of class A drugs such as morphine and diamorphine. The Victoria Climbié case in 2002 led to a review of social care when Victoria was entrusted by her parents to stay with her great-aunt who subsequently abused and tortured her to death (Littlemore, 2003). A report into the case found a chain of neglect transcending health and social care and leading to a review of policies and procedures within the services.

The impact of these major failings and others has resulted in a lack of public confidence in the health service and a rise in the numbers of complaints proceeding to litigation (Wilson & Tingle, 1999).

Trend towards greater access to care information

The advances in information technology, for example the Internet, has resulted in an easier access to information by the public. Individuals are able to access the same information as healthcare professionals, for example the Cochrane Library and Department of Health website, empowering and informing the public with specific information relating to their condition. This ability to access information, which was perhaps difficult to obtain previously, is fuelling the public's demands and expectations for quality care. Health and social care professionals need to be aware of these rising expectations along with the Freedom of Information Act (DH, 2003), which has made access to healthcare information easier. Furthermore, websites like Doctor Foster (www.drfoster.co.uk), National Electronic Library for Health (NeLH) (www.nelh.nhs.uk) and Public Patient Involvement (DH, 2003) reinforce the need for professionals to be aware of giving, receiving and sign-posting patients and carers to the relevant sources of information. Healthcare professionals also need to be aware of other important factors that may impact on accessing and sharing information such as increased patient dependency and advanced technology.

Professional

Professional accountability

Case study 2.1 Professional practice: its relevance to excellence in health and social care

During a period of induction a newly qualified physiotherapist asked the mentor what were the key professional factors that might impact or compromise a health and social care professional's accountability.

The mentor responded by stating that there were several factors emerging that might impact or compromise health and social care professionals' accountability. These are associated increased professional accountability, patient dependency, advanced technology and the rise in litigious activities.

For more information about the drivers impacting and compromising professional accountable practice, read the remainder of this section.

All health and social care professionals are expected to account for their practice (General Medical Council, 2001; Health Professions Council, 2003; Nursing & Midwifery Council, 2004; General Social Care Council, 2006). The government (DH, 1997) and professional bodies recognise the significance of Cochrane's (1979) early work associated with ensuring their practice is supported with evidence. This is evident in professional bodies' codes of professional practice and conduct where a need for efficient and effective intervention with the backing of evidence is required. Even more disquieting is the fact that patients are increasingly holding professionals accountable for their care. Today registered nurses (indeed all health and social care professionals) are professionally accountable for the effectiveness of the care they provide (Lo Biondo-Wood & Haber, 1990). Professional accountability within the context of evidence-based practice reinforces the need for health and social care professionals to practise within the sphere of the standards set by their professional bodies. Furthermore, accountability according to Dimond (1995) extends beyond professional practice. All health and social care professionals in exercising their duty of care are ultimately accountable to the public through criminal law, to their employer through contract law and contract of employment and job description, and finally to the patient through a duty of care in common and civil law. The contract of employment reinforces the need for the health and social care professional as well as all staff to maintain their professional accountability by outlining their roles and responsibilities within the job description. Parties agree the contract of employment with the assumption that the employee will perform their duties according to professional, organisational and local policies and procedures, these being based on sound evidence (Sheldon & Parker, 1997; Thompson, 1999; Kuokkanen & Leino-Kilpi, 2000). Furthermore, as part of professional accountability it is important that health and social care professionals maintain their knowledge, skills and competency in practice. This can only be achieved by focusing attention on continued professional development (CPD) and life-long learning (LLL).

Increased patient dependency

The increased numbers of an ageing population means that patients are admitted into acute and community hospitals with far more complex physical and social problems (McSherry, 1999), requiring timely, appropriate interventions from a wide range of health and social care practitioners. For example, the average length of stay in acute hospital following total hip replacement surgery has gone down from fourteen to seven days, attributed to multi-disciplinary and cross-agency collaborative working. A further example is in the advances in stroke care and rehabilitation and in the establishment of specialist stroke units where the evidence (Stroke Unit Trialists' Collaboration, 1998) clearly demonstrates that recovery is better if these patients are managed in a specialist unit and not on an acute general medical ward. The major effect of increases in dependency levels has resulted in the need for greater efficiency, for example in maximising lengths of stay and maintaining high levels of acute bed occupancy. However, the shorter average lengths of patient stay seem to suggest that effective discharge planning is lessened due to staff having less planning time (particularly in complex social cases). Re-admission rates may have increased and certainly higher and greater demands are made of the community nursing services, hospital at home schemes, continuing and long-term care facilities, as more patients with complex physical and social needs require continued health and social care.

Advances in care technology

Advances in health and social care technology have made inroads in improving the quality and standards of care delivery, for example pressure-relieving equipment, moving and handling equipment, medical administration and monitoring equipment and wound care management, all having the potential for enhancing the quality of care delivered by health and social care professionals. However, credentialisation (demonstrating the evidence that staff have the knowledge, competence and skills to use the equipment safely) may be questionable. The downside is allowing the staff time and resources for education and training to use the equipment in an ever demanding and stressful clinical environment. The latter should not be the case if clinical governance is implemented successfully. These identified pressures being placed upon health and social care professionals to deliver a high quality service based upon appropriate evidence have the potential to create a conflict between balancing efficiency, and effectiveness and maintaining quality and standards. These aspirations cannot be achieved for all patients and carers without adequate resourcing and government backing and by some cultural changing.

Rising numbers of complaints going to litigation

Over the past decade we have witnessed a huge rise in the numbers of formal complaints made by patients and carers about hospital and community services proceeding to litigation. The National Heath Service Litigation Authority (NHSLA) paid out £502.9 million for clinical negligence claims in 2004–2005 compared with £422.5 million for 2003–2004 (NHSLA, 2005). These claims could be associated with the following:

• increased activity levels of health and social care
• greater propensity to pursue a complaint to litigation
• increased compensations for negligence claims (more likely to seek redress when something goes wrong) if outcome that can result in monetary gain.

It is worth noting here that the vast majority of complaints are resolved at a local level, often with clarification, explanations and the occasional apology when things have gone wrong. Honesty and openness are the key principles to deal with complaints, as well as developing robust mechanisms for the sharing of information to deal with issues before they become problems (McSherry, 1996). Management needs to encourage a learning culture, which proactively rather than reactively responds to seek redress when something goes wrong. The ultimate aim is to have a blame-free culture that encourages nurses to openly report, discuss and learn from clinical incidents or clinical complaints. In many instances complaints arise from systems failures rather than the actions or omissions of individuals. Healthcare professionals need to be made aware of this situation and have the knowledge, skills, competence and confidence to positively deal with complaints.

Conclusion

There are many contributing factors driving the need for health and social care professional teams and organisations to provide excellence in practice. Undoubtedly more factors will continue to arise reinforcing the need for the continuous search for excellence in practice in the future. These are explored in more detail in the next chapter.

Key points

- No single factor has led to the government's current position for modernisation, improvement or system reform of health and social cares services in the quest for excellence in practice.
- Political drivers for excellence in practice should be viewed with both a capital and small 'p'. The capital 'P' refers to those drivers resulting directly from government and policy. The small 'p' relates to organisation and personal factors that influence change and policy decision-making at a local level.
- Taking into account the many recent policy changes within health and social care a way forward to achieving excellence in care is by manifesting a vision through encouraging participation, partnership building and working in order to change perceptions of staff and public in order to achieve a state of professionalism.
- The social model is ideal for achieving excellence in care because it transcends professional disciplines focusing on stakeholder networking from the diverse range of services and individuals who come in contact with adults and children. The emphasis is placed on multi-disciplinary and shared working relationships which continue to place the patient at the centre of care.
- The media continues to play a major role in increasing patients' and carers' awareness of the NHS through the publication of clinical successes and failures in the organisations.
- All health and social care professionals are expected to account for their practice.
- The vast majority of complaints are resolved at a local level, often with clarification, explanations and the occasional apology for when things have gone wrong. Honesty and openness are the key principles to deal with complaints.

 Activity 2.2 Feedback

The contributing factors driving for excellence in health and social care practice can be attributed to the following:

- Changes in health policy
- The impact of organisational change on the provision and delivery of health care
- Rising patient and public expectations and involvement
- Demographic changes
- Lack of public confidence in healthcare provision due to media coverage of poor clinical practices
- Trend towards greater access to healthcare information
- Increased patient dependency
- Advances in healthcare technology
- Rising numbers of complaints going to litigation

A closer review of the above factors demonstrates three primary drivers that collectively form the 'three p' approach to clinical governance: Political, Professional and Public.

Further reading

McSherry, R., Pearce, P. (2007) *Clinical Governance: A Guide to Implementation for Healthcare Professionals*, 2nd edn. Blackwell Science: Oxford.

Useful links

Department of Health (2005) *Every Child Matters*. http:// www.everychildmatters.gov.uk/ (accessed 8 August 2007).

References

Allsop, J. (1986) *Health Policy and The National Health Service*. Longman: London.
Bristol Royal Infirmary Inquiry (2001) The Report of the Public Inquiry into Children's Heart Surgery at the Bristol Royal Infirmary 1984–1995: Learning from Bristol. CM 5207 (I). HMSO: London.
Cochrane, A. (1979) *Effectiveness and Efficiency Random Reflections on the Health Service*. Nuffield Provisional Hospital Trust: Leeds.
Department of Health (1989) White Paper: *Working for Patients*. DH: London.
Department of Health (1991) *Health of the Nation*. DH: London.
Department of Health (1992) *Raising the Standards*. DH: London.
Department of Health (1993) *The Citizens Charter*. DH: London.
Department of Health (1997) *The New NHS Modern and Dependable*. DH: London.
Department of Health (1998a) *Quality in the New NHS*. DH: London.
Department of Health (1998b) Reducing junior doctors' continuing action to meet new deal standards rest periods and working arrangements, improving catering and accommodation for juniors, other action points. Health Services Circular 1998/240. DH: London.
Department of Health (2000a) *The NHS Plan: A Plan for Investment, a Plan for Reform*. DH: London.
Department of Health (2000b) *National Service Framework for Coronary Heart Disease: Modern Standards and Service Models*. DH: London.
Department of Health (2000c) Freedom of Information Act 2000. http:// www.dh.gov.uk/PublicationsAndStatistics/FreedomOfInformation/FreedomOfIn-formationAct2000/fs/en?CONTENT_ID=4055574&chk=KOAYUH
Department of Health (2001) Major cash boost for mental health services. http:// www.dh.gov.uk/PublicationsAndStatistics/PressReleases/PressReleasesNotices/fs/ en?CONTENT_ID=4011514&chk=dUYGu/
Department of Health (2003) http://www.dh.gov.uk/PublicationsAndStatistics/ PressReleases/PressReleasesNotices/fs/en?CONTENT_ID=4062851&chk=/YNcaY
Department of Health (2004) European working time directive. http://www.dh.gov.uk/ PolicyAndGuidance/HumanResourcesAndTraining/WorkingDifferently/European-WorkingTimeDirective/fs/en
Department of Health (2006) *Our Health, Our Care, Our Say*. DH: London.
Dimond, B. (1995) *Legal Aspects of Nursing*, 2nd edn. Prentice Hall: Inglewood Cliffs, NJ.
General Medical Council (2001) *Good Medical Practice*. GMC: London.
General Social Care Council (2006) *Codes of Practice for Social Care Workers and Employers*. GSCC, London. http://www.gscc.org.uk (accessed 22 November 2007).

Griffiths, R. (1983) *NHS Management Enquiry*. DHSS: London.

Ham, C. (1986) *Health Policy in Britain*. Macmillan: London.

Health Professions Council (2003) *Standards of Conduct, Performance and Ethics. Your Duties as a Registrant 2003*. HPC: London.

HMSO (2002) Statutory Instrument 2002 No. 3048. http://www.opsi.gov.uk/si/si2002/20023048.htm

Jarrold, K. (2005) Being a better manager. *Health Service Journal* 8 December: 35.

Kuokkanen, L., Leino-Kilpi, H. (2000) Power and empowerment in nursing: three theoretical approaches. *Journal of Advanced Nursing* 31(1): 235–41.

Lancet (1998) Editorial: First lessons from the 'Bristol Case'. 351(9117): 1669.

Littlemore, S. (2003) Victoria Climbié: Chain of Neglect. BBC News: London. http://bbc.co.uk/1/low/uk/2700427.stm (accessed 22 November 2007).

Lo Biondo-Wood, G., Haber, J. (1990) *Nursing Research: Methods, Critical Appraisal and Utilization*. C.V. Mosby: Toronto.

McNeil, J. (1998) Clinical governance: the whys, whats, and hows for theatre practitioners. *British Journal of Theatre Nursing* 9(5): 208–16.

McSherry, R. (1996) Multidisciplinary approach to patient communication. *Nursing Times* 92(8): 42–3.

McSherry, R. (1999) Supporting patients and their families. In: Bassett, C.C., Makin, L. *Caring for the Seriously Ill Patient*. Arnold: London.

McSherry, R. (2004) Practice development and health care governance: a recipe for modernisation. *Journal of Nursing Management* 12: 1–10.

McSherry, R., Haddock, J. (1999) Evidence based health care: Its place within clinical governance. *British Journal of Nursing* 8(2): 113–17.

McSherry, R., Johnson, S. (2005) (eds) *Demystifying the Nurse/Therapist Consultant: A Foundation Text*. Nelson Thornes: Cheltenham,.

McSherry, R., Pearce, P. (2007) *Clinical Governance: A Guide to Implementation for Healthcare Professionals*, 2nd edn. Blackwell Publishing: Oxford.

National Statistics (2004) http://www.statistics.gov.uk/cci/nugget.asp?id=881

NHSLA (2005) http://www.nhsla.com/Claims/

Nursing and Midwifery Council (2004) *The NMC Code of Professional Conduct. Standards for Conduct, Performance and Ethics*. NMC: London.

Press Association (2005) Obesity levels continue to rise. *Guardian* 16 December.

Stroke Unit Trialists' Collaboration (1998) Organised inpatient (stroke unit) care after stroke. In: Warlow, C., van Gijn, J., Sandercock, P. (eds) Stroke Module of the Cochrane Database of Systematic Reviews. BMJ Publishing Group: London.

Sheldon, L., Parker, P. (1997) The power to lead. *Nursing Management* 4(1): 8–9.

Shipman Inquiry (2005) The Shipman Inquiry. HMSO: London. http://www.the-shipman-imquiry.org.uk/finalreport.asp

Thompson, C. (1999) A conceptual treadmill: The need for 'middle ground' in clinical decision making theory in nursing. *Journal of Advanced Nursing* 30(5): 1222–9.

Wilkinson, G., Miers, M. (1999) *Power and Nursing Practice*. Macmillan: London.

Wilson, J., Tingle, J. (1999) *Clinical Risk Modification: A Route to Clinical Governance*. Butterworth Heinemann: Oxford.

3 Excellence in context: contemporary health and social care

Introduction

The context in which health and social care is delivered has a critical effect on the ability to deliver a quality service. Excellence in practice is not restricted to one's personal behaviour, professional competence or the overall service delivery within a unit. All care is further regulated within additional frameworks and legislation from the local employer, through national administration and legislation to global considerations. This wider context reflects political, as well as clinical, imperatives and aspirations and puts the individual's practice within a complex network of guidance and regulation (Dargie, 1999). This, then, provides the framework by which an integrated service can be provided, regulated and managed. It has been suggested by Page & Hamer (2002:11) that there are four primary levels for consideration within such a strategic context and that they all require attention in developing practice:

- Individual
- Intra-organisational, e.g. ward/department/unit
- Organisational, e.g. hospital or primary care trust
- Supra-organisational, e.g. regional, national, international.

This may have the effect of creating tensions as expectations and objectives vary between level considerations. This is particularly in evidence in regard to financial considerations within service delivery. By its nature, care and its ability to provide quality of delivery is, at its most fundamental level, economically driven. The onus is, therefore, on professional practice and services to deliver within these constraints and be accountable for the care that is provided. The practitioner who seeks to develop excellence in practice needs to fully appreciate what these influences are, develop skills of critical consideration and utilise them to guide and substantiate their everyday working. In this way there is the potential for a truly integrated and excellent service of care delivery irrespective of the focus or setting.

 Activity 3.1 Reflective question

Outline what you think are the major influences you need to consider when seeking to promote excellence in your own area of practice.

Read on and compare your answers with Figures 3.1 and 3.5.

Organisational arrangements and culture

According to Mehl (1993) achieving excellence in individual, team and organisational development can be based on nine considerations which we have expanded for application in health and social care as shown in Figure 3.1.

- **Political and social norms:** where the service delivery reflects the philosophy, values and needs of the society in which it operates
- **Standards of practice:** determined at a variety of levels reflecting education, skill development and regulatory frameworks
- **Available resources:** which try to balance need and demand through the provision of personnel, equipment and other resources to assist care delivery
- **Perceptions:** including those of the service user, professional and other staff delivering care, managers and policy makers as well as the general public
- **Time:** both for delivery of care as well as personal and team developments. It reflects multiple demands on the role
- **Motivation to progress to a higher level:** thus ambitions and aspirations to improve and develop affect both the individual and the whole team
- **Continuous innovation:** an emphasis on the principles of practice development to incorporate service development and evaluation in a meaningful way
- **Reshaping professions:** avoiding the 'tribalism' and restrictive practices which work against patient-centred approaches
- **Meeting the needs of society:** through adherence to professional practice and reflecting responsibilities and accountability for that practice

Figure 3.1 Key considerations to achieving excellence in practice

The range of service considerations in Figure 3.1 offers a challenging list of demands. Within the UK, and many other developed countries with a comprehensive health and social care service, the model of planning and regulatory management is increasingly becoming one of centralised rather than local planning and drives change through comprehensive legislation which constantly has an impact on front-line services and the individual's practice. Similarly, the service is frequently reported on by a voracious media industry which often displays a preoccupation with how services are delivered and new developments, frequently from a very critical stance. There does not, at times appear to be any limit to the public appetite for such health and social care-related articles. This is not surprising, however, when the service is funded either individually by fee, or collectively through taxation, and therefore health and social care delivery and its management affects these 'consumers' at the most fundamental and individual level (DH, 2000). Individual health, or lack of it, affects every component of our existence and ability to function in all areas of life. This generally means that the patient or service user is particularly interested in these services as they can have such a direct effect on one's sense of well-being. For the people who deliver services, as a recipient of public (or private) funding to deliver care, there is also a need to be accountable for the service provided as with any other service that the public might access. This chapter, therefore, acts as an introduction to the context of health and social care and the key influences and issues. By exploring some of the important contemporary issues associated with achieving excellence in care and how they can be utilised in a positive way it provides an understanding to assist in the improvement and development of quality practice and service delivery. The emphasis is on highlighting the following: national targets and performance management, the use of National Service Frameworks (NSFs), enhancing public confidence, building partnerships and collaborative working, as well as improving access to information through sharing and networking

National targets and performance management

Centralised management of services tends to be heavily dependent on setting and measuring comprehensive targets applicable to all local care providers. National targets are an embodiment of service aims and aspirations presented as centrally determined statements of objectives. Their intention is to set a benchmark for services, which all must achieve, and a key feature of performance management approaches. They have been increasingly used to guide the delivery of care within the National Health Service.

A patient-focused NHS is a service that exists **for** the patient and which is designed to meet the needs and wishes of the individual receiving care and treatment (DH, 2000).

The above statement represents the aspirations and challenges of developing excellence in practice through a more patient focused approach within the context of contemporary health and social care. It illustrates, however, that there is potential for a tension between individualist service provision and collective models of organisation to deliver it. Practice, as previously outlined, does not occur in a vacuum; it is guided and regulated by the context influences in which it operates. It is also, due to these influences, constantly in processes of change which are increasingly being recognised as the realities of professional practice. There is increasing emphasis on target setting and performance management to deliver a comprehensive, individually responsive service within the constraints imposed upon it, in order to promote equity and meet increasing demands and expectations within finite resources (Hutton, 2006). Over the past 25 years in the UK *all* governments have had national targets linked to improvements in funding practices and addressing the needs of patients. The importance attached to this can readily be seen when one considers that the UK public sector spending, with health and social care as the main beneficiary, was £560 billion in 2005 and continues to grow (Hutton, 2006). Centralising of focus and decision-making increases accountability in many levels of a service but also requires tiers of management and control at each level to ensure acceptable and consistent implementation at the points of delivery and a comprehensiveness of a 'national service'. There is, often, also a requirement for some degree of local flexibility within such an example of a national framework, in order to respond to and meet the unique considerations or specific demands of a local population. Such a consideration can be seen in the formation of local commissioners of services such as primary care trusts, but operating within the context of a regulatory national framework. This is an approach to ensuring that the centralised targets can be met at the point of delivery but has the potential to increase variance between service providers and will be further discussed below.

Target setting

Advocates of centralised target setting believe that these explicit targets allow delivery of what people want from public services in a consistent and efficient manner and bring services closer to the people who use them (Hutton, 2006). They can also be viewed as a means to transform public services 'from monolithic institutions to flexible user-focused services' (Hutton, 2006). Used in performance management terms they promote audit and accountability of priorities due to the explicit nature of targets and the political and financial will to deliver them. They reflect the prevailing ideologies and embrace the philosophical as well as pragmatic political attitudes of the government in power (Dargie, 1999). An example to illustrate this is the formation of the National Health Service in the United Kingdom in 1947. Whilst the founding principles of the service can clearly be seen in Figure 3.2 and may be considered to continue to hold true, targeting has and will continue to change the emphasis of individual components and continue to interpret the service's aims in the light of change and developments.

- Collectivism
- Access for all citizens to all types of health services
- Universal principle: free at the point of use
- Founded by National Insurance and general taxation
- Equality
- Principle of professional autonomy

Figure 3.2 Founding principles of the UK NHS in 1948 (Allsop, 1984)

It can easily be seen that such principles require interpretation and will generally represent the prevailing view on the way(s) services can meet those aims in a current context. An increasingly important embodiment and thus a driver of these aims is through 'targeting' priorities, which can either reflect health aims such as reduction in heart disease, or through service or managerial issues such as reduction of waiting times for appointments and consultations. Whilst not mutually exclusive both can be derived from different interpretations of priorities and principles. Good targets are generally those that are driven by consumer demands, give specific direction for change, are measurable and identify and link to other areas for change.

They can, therefore, also have a significant role in their capacity to stimulate excellence in services. Critics have suggested that central, all-inclusive targeting, is unrealistic unless it works closely with the patient and, therefore, that a key feature of a target is its acceptability (NHS Scotland, 2002). By reflecting controversial or poorly negotiated priorities targets may have the opposite effect to that intended, creating divides and detrimentally affect 'non-targeted' areas (National Audit Office, 2004). To avoid 'target overburden' there is, at present, a movement towards setting fewer comprehensive national targets and towards an increase in locally determined priorities through health plans and commissioning of services guided by local need. Centralised direction remains as a guide to these processes and will continue to act as a cornerstone of the performance management of both the whole service and individual practice of care-givers in order to demonstrate efficiency and effectiveness of the whole service.

Demonstrating efficiency and effectiveness

Both health and social care, as publicly funded services, are constantly being asked to not only meet service demands within finite resources, but also to demonstrate that these services are delivered in the most efficient and effective ways. Targeting, as discussed, is one strategy of centralised control to guide and measure these requirements. Targets are an effective, albeit blunt, way of achieving and measuring service changes in terms of efficiency and effectiveness. Efficiency, in care terms, can be viewed as achieving desirable outcomes, maximising the output from finite resources: being 'fit for purpose' (Jones, 1994:541). It also embodies a utilitarian philosophy; that is, providing the maximum 'good' for the largest part of a population. This 'most benefit' model will be achieved at the expense of some individual need for collective good and thus is frequently open to criticism in elements of human services where individualism is valued (Dargie, 1999). Effectiveness, by comparison, holds that something can be said to work. This is a contentious statement as it will only be evaluated, however, on the criteria specifically applied and therefore can only be judged against what measure it can be said to work. This suggests that there is potential for a myriad of different views on what effectiveness is. These will vary depending on the perspective applied and it is useful to view it as a range of focuses and therefore different ways of assessing or measuring it. Culyer (1991) provides a view of several types of efficiency which can be categorised into several key areas (Figure 3.3).

- Providing only services that are effective
- Providing services at minimum cost
- Concentrating resources on effective services
- Providing a mix of services to ensure benefits are justified by increased costs

Figure 3.3 Types of efficiency

It can be seen from Figure 3.3 that competing views of efficiency could compromise the agreed direction for a service as well as acting directly against the development of excellence in all respects. This can be illustrated through the evaluation of treatments in terms of efficiency. One way of driving efficiency is by only sanctioning 'evidence-based' treatments and approaches. This is a problematic concept as evidence is frequently judged on the average effect on a population, rather than individual efficacy as within the widely used and highly valued results of research using randomised controlled trials (Rolfe, 1999). This aggregated effect will give a single measure for judgement of effectiveness and can overlook atypical or individual effects which are at variance with this mean effect. Despite this, central decision-making based on evaluation of evidence has become a key determinant of acceptable approaches, despite its being clearly representative of one approach to efficiency when applied to a service. This dominant paradigm has resulted in a formalised process for evaluating evidence for utilisation in practice.

Evaluating evidence for practice

The National Institute for Health and Clinical Excellence (NIHCE), formerly the National Institute for Clinical Excellence, is an example of the adoption of this approach and is clearly founded on the principles of evaluating treatments (NICE, 2001) against standards of efficiency and effectiveness. Its primary purpose is to set a benchmark for evidence-based practice utilising the work of Cochrane (1972) and make recommendations for utilisation of treatments and care approaches. Its approach is by consideration of the evidence base for a treatment or intervention based on the 'strength of evidence' embodied in a hierarchy of research approaches that emphasise maximum benefits (see Figure 3:4). Practitioners are expected to base their practice on such evidence but also need to be informed 'consumers' and generators of other forms of evidence in relation to their practice (Rycroft-Malone et al., 2004). There is increasing emphasis on the skills required to critically analyse published research and practice development studies as well as utilising sound theoretical frameworks to guide and substantiate the care given. A challenge for future excellence in practice is to increase the volume and opportunities available to aid dissemination of local initiatives as well as larger scale research studies. The challenge for many health and social care professionals is undertaking research that is recognised within this hierarchy of evidence (Muir-Gray, 1997). See Figure 3.4.

- Experimental studies, e.g. randomised controlled trials
- Quasi-experimental studies, i.e. no randomisation
- Controlled observational studies
- Observational studies without control groups
- Expert opinion

Figure 3.4 Hierarchy of evidence

'Excellence' suggests an inclusive approach guided by both efficiency and effectiveness in utilising robust targets and standards to enhance professional practice. By being more transparent in its processes than clinical judgement alone, it can be seen to have the capacity to empower individuals, particularly patients and service users and promote the taking of responsibility for care by promoting internal quality assurance programmes. Patients and service users are becoming more involved as consumers and will continue to be better informed than previous generations due to the accessibility of information and engagement with services and this will require more collaborative ways of providing services. 'Rights' in health care is an increasingly cited demand on a service and with rights naturally go responsibilities affecting both care-givers and the patient in maintaining health and managing illness. To reconcile these possible tensions clarity is a key requirement and this requires emphasis on good care, practice and service delivery. Aids to assist the development of efficient and effective care are outlined in Figure 3.5.

- Clear and agreed organisational values
- Measures of quality
- Management
- Communication

Figure 3.5 Aids to efficient and effective care

These aids to efficient and effective service delivery can help to provide a 'culture' in which best practice can be fostered and a receptive vehicle for delivering agreed 'best practice' based on evidence and acceptability. Such an approach moves away from crude targeting alone towards adoption of excellent models of care such as National Service Frameworks.

National Service Frameworks (NSFs)

The NSFs were launched in 1988 as a rolling programme of policy and guidance for aspects of care. They are long-term strategies for improving specific areas of care by setting measurable goals within prescribed time frames (DH, 2006). They differ from national governmental targets by bringing together health and social care professionals, service users and carers, service managers, partner agencies and other advocates as an External Reference Group to determine best practice through engaging the full range of views. In essence the NSFs set national standards and identify key interventions for a defined service or care group; put in place strategies to support implementation; establish ways to ensure progress within an agreed timescale; form one of a range of measures to raise quality and decrease variations in service (DH, 2006).

NSFs aid the promotion of excellence through practice development by recognising the wider context of care delivery and prioritising, defining and guiding national standards to which all services should adhere. Standards are designed to not only protect the public from harm but to ensure that care is both appropriate, achievable and of an acceptable quality. They embrace efficiency and effectiveness by sharing best practice and giving vision. They also represent 'best evidence' in practice. In so doing, they have the capacity to better meet user expectations and ensure that the same level of (quality) care is delivered consistently, particularly by allowing the standards to be audited. Thus they also increase the accountability of service deliverers and enhance the confidence that the public rightly expects.

Enhancing public confidence through building partnerships

Where there is greater participation and involvement of all parties such as in NSFs there is a greater sense of partnership and consequent confidence in the results. Previous models tended to favour the notion of 'expertness' and 'knowing what is best for another'. Increasingly there is an emphasis on person- or patient-centredness as the approach to partnership. This has been described as 'the standing that is bestowed upon one human being by another in the context of a relationship and social being. It implies recognition, respect and trust' (Kitwood, 1997:8). Expert authority and paternalistic models of health and social care are, therefore, increasingly being challenged and replaced as the guiding principle of service delivery through the increasing emphasis on the patient focus and a greater extent of public involvement (Dargie, 1999). Public expectations are higher than they have ever been and there is a drive for greater public and community involvement in care planning and delivery, with an increased risk of litigation for less than perfect services. The reality of partnerships has moved away from 'tokenistic' consultation to a changed relationship of real partnership and progressive growth of services offered by a range of providers within a united service offering approaches to maintaining health and preventing and managing illness. Charters, standards, targets and service specifications are additional representations of this changing culture and emphasis on partnership working (Figure 3.6).

Partnership working is also a key issue in successful inter-profession and inter-agency working in the delivery of care services. By clear collaboration,

 Activity 3.2 Reflective question

You are approached by a service manager to explore the experiences of staff and patients in improving how care is delivered.

Describe how you would ensure that the work was supported by the principles of effective partnership working.

Read on and compare your answers with the findings at the end of the chapter.

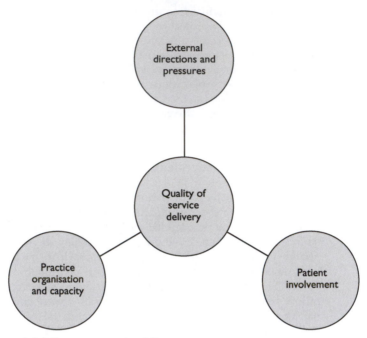

Figure 3.6 Influences on service delivery

cooperation and team approaches with a distinct patient/client focus it is possible to avoid service fragmentation and provide an integrated or 'seamless service'.

Figure 3.7 outlines recognised areas of focus that assist the production of a 'seamless service'.

Reducing divisions in care, e.g. between health and social care and other agencies through clear communication, cooperation and clarity about responsibilities.
Encouraging multi-professional working by reducing professional divisions and 'siloing' along traditional models of roles and responsibilities.
Realising potential by encouraging innovation, flexibility, new ways of working and professional cooperation within accepted responsibilities and accountabilities required by professional regulation.
Public engagement through informing, educating, involving and consulting with the actual and potential users who pay for the service and have rights and expectations of it.

Figure 3.7 Recognised areas of focus that assist the production of a 'seamless service'

It is evident from Activity 3.1 and the above requirements that both the public and staff have a right to demand collaborative, safe, quality, effective and efficient care delivered in a transparent manner. Much of the emphasis also has moved towards 'healthy living' partnerships, promotion of health and education. Most importantly it puts the patient at the centre of the process as outlined in the Department of Health's *A Stronger Local Voice* document (DH, 2006). This is an explicit drive towards patient-led services, with agreed targets and measures of performance, led and delivered through bottom-up approaches (DH, 2006). This is also the aim of preventative health strategies and links with public health initiatives, which require collaboration to promote health and well-being and reduce illness and barriers to community welfare. All of these depend, however, on close collaborative working, particularly with the recipients of caring services.

Promoting collaborative working

The principles of excellent practice require that the service user is always at the centre of care in a very real way and that there is a genuine team approach within a positive care model. As Tingle (2007:1034) rightly states: 'the patient is to be king in the new NHS'. In partnership working based on 'informed, shared, decision-making and governance' patients and health workers are being encouraged to recognise the primacy of the patient in developing 'quality contracts' to inform and guide healthcare (Delbanco et al., 2001:144). Historically there has also tended to be a 'silo' effect as each profession or aspiring profession defends and develops its perceived role in the care delivery at the expense of joint working or consideration of the best responses to meet patient needs. Increasingly there is an emphasis on designing the optimal 'patient journey' (Bauman et al., 2003; Jeffries & Chan, 2004; RCN, 2005; Wales, 2005) and matching the most appropriate skills to the needs at each stage.

> A whole patient journey is a dynamic, locally agreed patient-centred approach which crosses organisational and primary/secondary care boundaries. The pathway is developed by the multidisciplinary team, which includes strong patient/carer involvement, using the best evidence to guide practice (City Hospitals Sunderland NHS Foundation Trust, in Campbell et al., 2006).

When undertaken with full recognition of this patient-centredness there is an inevitable and visible change in how care is given, by whom and in ways that foster timeliness and efficiency and effectiveness. To achieve this requires whole service development and it is vital that teams are committed to such approaches and that 'tribalism' is sacrificed for the benefits of col-laborative working. This is a demanding challenge to services and requires hard work by all team members within a responsive and open approach.

Case study 3.1 demonstrates that in order to resolve this practical problem it is imperative that the team develop and work effectively using several key elements to ensure this happens in reality. These are consultation and patient-focus, communication, trust, openness, responsiveness, involve-ment. The approach is based on a philosophy that the journey through a

Case Study 3.1 Effective team working

Professor Steve Campbell and his team has used a 'patient journey' approach to develop collaboration within multidisciplinary teams towards patient centredness at the City Hospitals Sunderland NHS Trust. This involves intensive team working over a six-month period to evaluate and redesign existing healthcare provision within existing resources for specified client groups. The aim of the process is to provide a new and improved patient journey agreed by the whole team which delivers patient-centred, evidence-based healthcare for all patients within that clinical setting. For more details see Campbell et al. (2006).

service and its effect on the user is the best way to utilise the whole team within an integrated model of care. It also encourages sharing of information both within the service and outside of it. The ways in which the team access and share information between themselves and the patient is a key priority in developing excellence in a service and requires careful consideration.

Improving access to information through sharing and networking

'Better information, better choices, better health' is the stated policy and strategy of the modernisation of the health service (DH, 1997). There is a perceivable revolution in the ways that people access information in today's society. Communication opportunities through a wide variety of media have never been greater but with this comes the need for accuracy and accessibility of appropriate information to avoid confusion and 'information overload'. People make choices about their health every day in terms of what to eat or whether they exercise, as well as choices about whether or not to consult the doctor or care for themselves at home. 'Now, more so than ever before, patients are involved in making choices about their treatment' (Gann, 2005).

Better informed patients should not be viewed as a threat to professional status and should not cause anxieties if greater knowledge is perceived as a threat to the professional role. These paternalistic concerns can only be overcome within true partnership working where respect and best practice are keystone principles. For the professionals delivering care there are advantages to this increased information and the opportunities to consult and network if these concerns are overcome. Network opportunities are readily available through a range of media but are not always fully exploited by busy professionals. Some examples include:

- Public Health – all sectors
- Health Development Agency
- Condition specific groups

- NSFs
- Professional forums e.g. the Developing Practice Network—known today as Developing Subscribers Area FONS.
- Informal contact and 'professional conversations'
- Research and dissemination
- Partnership working
- Expert patient groups
- Practice development.

Conclusion

Practice does not occur in a vacuum and the wider context in which care is provided will have a major impact on that delivery. As deliverers of services we have responsibilities not only to our patients and colleagues but to the wider society in which we live and work. The care we give is only one part of an integrated and regulated service which will constantly re-prioritise the service. As professionals we can influence these priorities as well as recognising how our practice is influenced by this wider context. At its most fundamental, excellence in care can be provided through a recognition of these factors and the need to consider them and incorporate them into care appropriately. Putting the patient at the centre of the service, however, is the key to achieving the reconciliation of these potentially conflicting demands and influences and promoting truly professional team care. Good team working is not easily achieved and the next chapter will explore ways in which these influences can effectively be considered and utilised in changing organisational cultures and developing ways of working in order to promote excellence.

 Activity 3.3   Feedback

The key to effective partnership building is ensuring the following:

- Clarity of purpose
- Open and honest communication
- Trust and cooperation
- Reducing divisions
- Encouraging innovation
- Collaboration and involvement
- Accepting individual and group responsibility
- Education, reflection and learning

Key points

- Practice exists in the wider context of political and social care
- Patient-centredness is vital if effective and efficient care is to be fostered

- Collaboration and partnership working are essential when combining professional responsibilities with seamless team working
- Communication and information are key to achieving excellent care standards
- Excellence requires standards both national and local and seeks to meet targets and demonstrate effectiveness and efficiency
- It is imperative to demonstrate performance as outcomes
- Care standards should be evaluated and audited

Further reading

Campbell, S., Watson, B., Gibson, A., Husband, G., Bremner, K. (2006) Comprehensive service and practice development: city hospitals. Sunderland's experience of patient journeys. *Practice Development in Health Care* 3:(1):15–26.

McCormack, B., Garbett, R. (2003) The characteristics, quality and skills of practice developers. *Journal of Clinical Nursing* 12: 317–25.

McSherry, R., Bassett, C. (2002) *Practice Development in the Clinical Setting: a Guide to Implementation*. Nelson Thornes: Cheltenham.

Useful links

Department of Health website: http://www.dh.gov.uk
Evidence Based Practice website: http://www.mdx.ac.uk/www/rctsh/ebp/main.htm
Foundation of Nursing Studies/Developing Practice Network: www.dpnetwork.org.uk
Patient perspective (including Expert Patient): http://www.nelh.nhs.uk/patient-centred.asp

References

Allsop, J. (1984) *Health Policy and the National Health Service*. Longman: London.

Bauman, A.E., Fardy, H.J., Harris, P.J. (2003) Getting it right: why bother with patient-centred care? *Medical Journal of Australia* 179: 253–6.

Campbell, S., Watson, B., Gibson, A., Husband, G., Bremner, K. (2006) Comprehensive service and practice development: city hospitals. Sunderland's experience of patient journeys. *Practice Development in Health Care* 3:(1):15–26.

Cochrane, A.L. (1972) *Effectiveness and Efficiency: Random Reflections on Health Services*. Nuffield Provincial Hospitals Trust: London.

Culyer, A. (1991) The promise of a reformed NHS: an economist's angle. *British Medical Journal* 302:1253–6.

Dargie, C. (ed.) (1999) *Policy Futures for UK Health*. Nuffield Trust: Oxford.

Delbanco, T., Berwick, D.M., Boufford, J.I., et al. (2001) Healthcare in a land called PeoplePower: nothing about me without me. *Health Expectations* 4: 144–50.

Department of Health (1997) *The New NHS: Modern and Dependable*. DH: London.

Department of Health (1998) *A First Class Service: Quality in the New NHS*. DH: London.

Department of Health (2000) *The NHS Plan*. DH: London.

Department of Health (2005) *National Service Frameworks (NSFs)* [online] www.dh.gov.uk/PolicyAndGuidance/HealthandSocialCareTopics

Department of Health (2006) *A Stronger Local Voice*. DH: London.

Gann, R. (2005) *NHS Direct. What is a good target?* Cabinet Office: London.

Jeffries, H., Chan, K.K. (2004) Multidisciplinary teamworking: is it holistic and effective? *International Journal of Gynaecological Cancer* 14: 210–11.

Hutton, T. (2006) On being a person. In: Kitwood, T. (ed.) *Dementia Reconsidered: the Person Comes First*. Open University Press: Milton Keynes.

Jones, L.J. (1994) *The Social Context of Health and Health Work*. Macmillan: Basingstoke.

Kitwood, T. (ed.) (1997) *Dementia Reconsidered: the Person Comes First*. Open University Press: Milton Keynes.

Mehl, B. (1993) Defining excellence. *American Journal of Hospital Pharmacy* 50(5): 921–8.

Muir-Gray, J.A. (1997) *Evidence-Based Health Care: How to Make Health Policy and Management Decisions*. Churchill Livingstone: New York.

National Audit Office (2004) *Public Sector Expenditure*. NAO: London.

National Health Service Scotland (2002) *Patient Focus and Public Involvement*. NHSS: Edinburgh.

National Institute for Clinical Excellence (2001) *The Guideline Development Process- Information for National Collaborating Centres and Guideline Development Groups*. NICE: London.

NHS Direct (2005) *Revolutionising Access to Health Information*. NHS Direct: London.

Page, S., Hamer, S. (2002) Practice development – time to realise the potential. *Practice Development in Health Care* 1(1): 2–17.

Rolfe, G. (1999) Insufficient evidence: the problems of evidence-based nursing. *Nurse Education Today* 19:433–42

Royal College of Nursing (2005) *Changing Patients' Worlds Through Nursing Practice Expertise: Exploring Nursing Practice Through Emancipatory Action Research and Fourth Generation Evaluation*. RCN: London.

Rycroft-Malone, J., Seers, K., Titchen, A., Harvey, G., Kitson, A., McCormack, B. (2004) What counts as evidence in evidence-based practice? *Nursing and Health Care Management and Policy* 47:(1):81–9.

Tingle, J. (2007) An introduction to clinical negligence; nurses and the law. *British Journal of Nursing* 11(15): 1033–5.

Wales, A. (2005) Managing knowledge to support the patient journey in NHS Scotland: strategic vision and practical reality. *Health Information and Libraries Journal* 22: 83–95.

4 Changing organisational cultures and working environments

Introduction

This chapter considers the importance of the organisation and its culture in the development of practice and the promotion of excellence. By drawing on some of the established organisational theories it seeks to consider the key elements for consideration in practical change strategies.

Against the background of the influences and considerations previously outlined, it can be seen that care organisations and services are complex structures embracing individuals collaborating and working together if satisfactory results are to be achieved as in the concepts of 'whole system thinking' (Checkland, 1981) and the 'learning organisation' (Senge, 1994). This emphasises the need to be both dynamic and responsive if the results reflect what the participants really care about and if excellence is the ambition and objective. It is easy and often comfortable to feel that the working environment would benefit from being in a state of stability and immune to change. This false and potentially damaging illusion was described by Schon (1987) suggesting that both society and institutions are continuously transforming. Thus theories which seek to describe or explain organisations tend to promote 'ideals' to which it strives and manages the fluidity of change through both its activities and processes (Finger & Brand, 1999). In healthcare such a fallacy of stability is especially acute because it overlooks the individuality of the participants and the need constantly to review and modify the ways in which care is provided. It does, however, emphasise the potential resistance that can occur if the complex whole of the system is unsettled in the presence of major change and particularly if unrecognised or poorly handled.

The organisation comprises a diversity of contributory roles and inputs. There is therefore a need to utilise these skills to develop practice and the team who provide it in order to embed a culture of striving for excellence in all aspects of the service. Theories of change management and leadership are helpful in managing these processes effectively and we have generally found that the starting point is a commonality of understanding allied to shared ambitions by the participants as in a whole system model (Senge, 1994). This translates in our context as sharing a vision and fostering joint values which give direction to the practice development process. A fundamental role in this is that of effective leadership and the skills of facilitation to clarify these concepts and develop ownership of the subsequent changes by the whole team and draws heavily on the team as a learning organisation.

This chapter continues with a review of some of the major considerations in changing organisations and working environments and identifies some key considerations for leading the changes and involving all those who receive and deliver care.

Need for diversity, equity and equality of services

We start this section on the premise that excellence is founded on the care service meeting the needs of a diverse population and the health and social problems. Essentially it is a collective service but which is individualised: a service for all; a service for the individual. It is important to explore the role of the organisational culture and its working environments in promoting excellence in practice that is founded on equity and equality in all facets of its operation. Excellent care is not offered as ready-made packages into which each individual must fit but by fostering an individualised patient-centred approach which is owned by the whole team and reflects professional and individual ambitions. This can be made explicit in the development of a working philosophy for the service to which all team members feel committed and which challenges practice based on ritual and routine. This enables a collective vision which can be supported by organisational frameworks to guide the activities and processes which foster best practice.

One framework specifically designed for this is that used for Practice Development Unit (PDU) accreditation schemes. Key requirements and standards, embodied in these PDU accreditation schemes enable an analysis of current working practices and give direction for future development against clear criteria and measurable objectives of achievement (Page et al., 1998) These will also be considered in more depth in Chapter 5 and further works in this series. A starting point for any care provider, however, is to develop an understanding of the whole organisation and its complex relationships in order to review current practices and reflect on areas for development. Reflections on practice are dependent on consideration of team 'styles' and approaches, managerial processes, the degree to which empowerment is facilitated and supported as well as the utilisation of individual and team strengths. All in all, the objective must be to promote both equity and individualism in the delivery of care within a consultative and partnership model of engagement.

 Activity 4.1 Reflective question

What organisational considerations would you undertake in your care setting before embarking on any strategy for innovation and change?

Read on and compare your answers with the information in Figures 4.1 and 4.2.

According to Activity 4.1 it is evident that before embarking on any form of innovation and change there are several important factors to consider that may enhance or inhibit the degree of success. In learning organisations ideal people behaviours have been suggested: team learning, shared visions, mental models, personal mastery and systems thinking (Senge, 1994). Recognition of these drivers of successful change and reductions of barriers can be an effective starting point for developing excellence in practice. Areas that a team might consider include:

- visioning and values
- traditional versus non-traditional working (rites and rituals)
- spirit of enquiry (analysis and review)
- willingness to change
- degree of patient centredness
- use of evidence and evidence-based practice
- health planning (utilising targets) health and sound planning
- user involvement
- hierarchical structure ('top-down and bottom-up')
- best practice sources and sharing.

These focus areas form the basis of many accreditation schemes and guide the team to critically analyse aspects of care which contribute to producing a model of practice where excellence can flourish. What Activity 4.1 also highlights is how the working environment of the organisation and culture really exert a major impact on any innovation or change processes.

Visioning and values

> In our work lives we are often seeking solutions to deal with ideas, problems and issues. Even the best solutions cannot work if the people involved do not support them (Lawless & Walsh, 2005:2).

The above quote from the Building Effective Engagement Techniques (BEET model, 2005) also emphasises the interpersonal and cooperative requirements in changing the way we work. It proposes a shared sense of beliefs made explicit through value and vision clarification. There are recognised deficiencies in all organisational theories (Finger & Brand, 1999) but it is generally accepted that successful cultures and organisations have a shared vision embodying corporate values and strategic objectives that are congruent with the vision and values of the individual members (Dixon, 1994). People will normally choose to work in an organisation and environment which explicitly confirms and validates the individual's beliefs, attitudes and behaviours. Thus dynamic health and social care settings are more likely to attract and retain dynamic staff members. Clarifying vision and values is an appropriate starting point for many care settings on their path to achieving excellence through the use of 'participative change cycles' (Hersey et al., 2001) and is reflected in the question outlined in Figure 4.1.

Part of the clarification process is reliant on determining the acceptable, desirable and ideal models of the service that are being delivered or could be

Consider the following questions both as an individual and by comparison with other team members:
- What are the aim(s) of the service?
- How do I contribute?
- What would an ideal service look like?
- What are my (our) values?
- What are my (our) vision(s)?
- How does our service relate to targets?
- How do we compare to best practice standards?

Figure 4.1 Clarifying vision and values

achieved and thus it also helps to clarify the individual's conception of professional practice. These discussions, emphasised as 'dialogue' (Gadamer, 1979) and genuine 'thinking together' (Senge, 1994), are key elements of whole system approaches and successful learning organisations and are evident in the way that most teams successfully reconsider the service and the ways that interprofessional/ disciplinary functioning helps or impedes patient-centred care in practice development approaches. Benchmarking using an existing model of quality can help to start these discussions, particularly where a team is relatively early in its working. There are many available in the literature as discussed in Chapter 1: Total Quality Management (TQM), Continuous Quality Improvement (CQI), Quality Circle, Clinical Pathways. A comparison of the different emphases of some approaches is shown in Table 4.1.

Developing teams through practice development is probably less important which one is selected compared with having shared criteria openly discussed and 'owned' by a team or organisation. Most models have similar areas of focus even if the emphasis differs. The elements of one approach is outlined below: Figure 4.2 (Maxwell, 1984) is one example of a model that supports innovation and change.

It is evident from Table 4.1 and Figure 4.2 that in seeking to achieve excellence in care it is essential to have a vision, a model of quality and a flexible but structured approach to innovation and change. Furthermore, it is important that this is linked to the organisational and strategic objectives

Table 4.1 Comparative models of quality for innovation and change

Safety, appropriateness, effectiveness and equality (WHO, 2005)	Fully meeting the needs of those who need the services most, at the lowest cost to the organisation (Ovretveit, 1990)
Continually improving patient care by minimising clinical risk and continuing the development of organisation and staff (McSherry & Pearce, 2002)	Education Clinical audit Risk management Research and development Openness (Starey, 2003)

- Relevance to need: Does the service adequately meet patient and staff needs?
- Effectiveness: Are patients getting the appropriate care in a timely and acceptable manner?
- Access to services: Are all services available when needed? Are they well integrated?
- Equity: Are all patients treated individually and equally?
- Social acceptability: Does the service meet expectations and requirements? Is accountability in evidence?
- Efficiency and economy: Does the process work? Could it be better? Is there a difference in cost?

Figure 4.2 Relevant questions derived from a model of quality by Maxwell (1984)

of the care service. This also should embrace explicit team and/or individual objectives and personal development plans (McSherry & Pearce, 2002). A team utilising learning organisation and whole systems approaches is likely to demonstrate the attributes outlined in Figure 4.3.

This sense of identity and ownership is more likely to encourage 'bottom-up' innovation and change through participation in contrast to top-down 'directive change cycles' (Hersey et al., 2001) where change is forced on the team through external force or higher management. In the participative model the team is more likely to take responsibility for the change, its reasons and its directions and effects.

Once there is greater clarity on the desired quality of the service, a vision, collective involvement and capacity to transform, the focus can move towards service integration and the individual member of the team's responsibilities. Integrated governance, a term introduced by McSherry & Pearce (2002), recognises and acknowledges that caring is a complex and multi-faceted process involving multiple stakeholders and users. The term incorporates key departments and systems such as informational, clinical, organisational, management, etc. The ultimate goal of integrated governance is about enhancing quality by providing excellence in individual and service practices through minimising risks and aiding the development of organisation and staff (McSherry & Pearce, 2002). It is generally divided into 'clinical', i.e. the actual care or treatment being delivered and 'shared', i.e. the roles and responsibilities of the team providing the care. The term integrated governance embraces both elements of clinical and shared governance under one umbrella term (Tingle, 2007).

- A sense of caring or passion
- Receptiveness to change/experimentation
- Valuing and rewarding learning
- Effective dialogue and communication
- Valuing individual and collective strengths
- Openness and trust
- Sense of responsibility and accountability

Figure 4.3 Qualities to assist a team striving for excellence in care

According to Tingle, integrated governance is the key vehicle for promoting quality care and in creating a working environment and culture in which excellence can flourish. Whilst Tingle (2007) and McSherry & Pearce (2002) may be correct in their views, some professionals continue to have difficulty in marrying these terms to the practice setting; so what do we mean by shared and/or clinical governance?

Shared governance

Organisations have responsibilities and collective accountability (Watkins & Marsick, 1992) as do the individuals who comprise that organisation. Much has been written on the individual professional's accountability, often embodied in codes of practice or professional guidance and regulation for the quality of practice, but corporate responsibility and 'shared governance' is a key feature of directly involving all personnel including the patient in ensuring quality of services. Recent inquiries (Health Ombudsman, 2005) have tended to emphasise a lack of corporate and team working in contributing to major failures of service delivery. In extreme cases, 'corporate manslaughter' is a sanction for legal redress in cases where loss of life results from failings in shared governance and this may be applied to health and social care in the future. Procedures and policies that are sanctioned by the employing authority are frequently determined in response to perceived or actual failings in a service but can be the result of a 'knee-jerk reaction' to an immediate problem rather than a considered view of the whole service. Excellence requires a shared sense of responsibility, quality of delivery and accountability in aspects of the service and is best fostered in an 'open and learning' organisation that values the involvement of all stakeholders in decision-making. By adopting the principles of shared governance (Figure 4.4) it is easy to see how excellence in care can be fostered at an individual, team and organisational level.

It is evident from Figure 4.4 that shared governance is as important in raising staff and public awareness of what and how the organisation can operate as it is to encourage and empower individuals to take responsibility

- Clarity of roles and responsibilities: this aids effective individual and team working
- Whole-team working: having a shared vision and sense of ownership
- Patient centredness; this informs and drives the service to meet needs
- Risk assessments: involving an appropriate balance of innovation with safety
- Management: having effective structures which support and facilitates practice
- Multi-professional learning: an openness to learning organisation principles to reduce 'tribalism' and foster team working
- 'No-blame' culture: this fosters trust and aids learning as well as acknowledging deficiencies
- Communication and trust: this emphasis on dialogue is a key to open team working
- Mutual respect: this is fostered through a recognition of the contribution of all participants

Figure 4.4 Principles of shared governance

for creating a philosophy and working ethos of excellence. However, the reality of achieving this in practical processes is often fraught with difficulty and challenge, which is why it requires a robust system to enable this to occur. Clinical governance is an ideal quality framework that enables this to occur at an individual, team and organisational level.

Clinical governance: a quality framework for excellence in care

A component of the corporate responsibility for 'governance' is the promotion and maintenance of sound, justifiable care and treatment. This combines the individual professional's sphere of practice and the concomitant responsibilities and accountabilities, with the overall team performance. It can foster pride and confidence in the skilled application of care within a supportive and open multidisciplinary model operating around the needs of the individual patient or client. Much practice is guided and regulated by professional bodies and councils through practice statements and directives but increasingly the 'scope and range' of practice and its governance rests within the judgement of the practitioner (Rycroft-Malone et al., 2004). This is supplemented by centralised guidance on efficacy of treatment and practice through research and clinical guidance, for example NIHCE discussed in the previous chapter. The importance of both NIHCE and clinical governance is the fact that they place the responsibility for providing excellent care with both the professional and the organisation by highlighting some important points for achieving quality (Activity 4.2).

 Activity 4.2　Personal evaluation

Using the following key principles for achieving quality care (NIHCE and clinical governance) consider what the following mean in relation to you and your team's roles:

- Duty of care
- Procedures and protocols
- Guidance and sanctions
- Clinical competence
- Education and training
- Updating knowledge and skills
- Professional judgement
- Evidence base for practice
- Legal, ethical and professional regulations
- Audit and research
- Management of incidents
- Professional responsibility
- Team responsibility
- Public perceptions

It is evident from Table 4.2 and Activity 4.2 that both shared and clinical governance offer the potential for a more integrated approach to supporting individuals, teams and organisations to achieve excellence in care. Excellence in care is also dependent on ensuring that all statutory, regulatory and policy guidance are evaluated in order to show performance and achievement of targets/outcomes. The latter can only be realised through developing robust systems of evaluation including quality audit(s). The findings from these can also be a major driver towards overcoming threats and recriminations and act as a tool for promoting care of the highest quality that is also justifiable and substantiated. By adopting the key principles of shared governance and using the clinical governance framework it is anticipated that the working of the organisation will be enhanced along with the quality experience of both public and professionals. This factor is further highlighted in the next section.

Importance of working environments and organisations

The realities of practice often include busy, stressful environments and demands on care-givers but are also perceived to be amongst the most rewarding professions and occupations in which to work (*Guardian* survey, 2006). There is obviously a need to strike a balance between these tensions as the degree to which the environment is supportive of quality care can relate to the perceptions and changes in circumstances acting on an individual. Maslow's classic representation of a hierarchy of needs (1968) is a useful reminder that the individual's ability to self-actualise (or perform optimally) is dependent on the satisfaction of lower order needs including safety and esteem needs. These can, therefore, act as both motivators for and detractors from optimum organisational and individual performance.

This highlights the need to address a range of both individual and collective elements in order to ensure that full potential can be achieved and thus promote improvements. In organisational terms this can also be applied as a guide for the team to ensure that all aspects of care for the patient or client address optimal criteria, but it equally applies to the team members as individuals and collectively, who will achieve their best, i.e. self-actualise, if all other hierarchical needs are met. An environment where a team member is affected by illness, where there are examples of poor care, or where the team is disunited will militate against the development of excellence. Apart from individual perceptions and experiences, consideration has to be given to the qualities of the setting within the context of care provision (macro-influences) and day-to-day care organisation and management (micro-influences). Good leadership and effective and responsive management is a key determinant to achieving change and progress. Yet effective leadership and management can be hampered by internal and external organisational influences that stem from individual and or organisational factors (Table 4.2).

Table 4.2 Examples of influences on individuals and organisations

Individual	Organisational
Internal	*Internal*
Feeling valued or not	Staff morale
Professional practice	Communication
Team membership	Sense of achievement
External	*External*
Professional guidance	Funding difficulties
Promotion prospects	Complaints
Financial constraints	Policy direction

The ways in which these influences are recognised and managed has a distinct bearing on the way teams work and how care is delivered. It is easy to see this in examples of care settings where the team works effectively within the prevailing demands to produce quality care, compared with others where the influences severely detract from the team's and organisation's ability to function in an effective manner. Some of the previously identified strategies, however, are known to particularly assist teams to remain functional and strive for quality even when under considerable pressures (Figure 4.5).

Figure 4.5 shows the need to both recognise and reconcile potentially damaging influences on care delivery and promote positive influences. This emphasises the importance of using these supportive factors to enhance innovation and change even when a team is under extreme pressure rather than creating or enabling negative responses to divert from excellence in practice. It is useful for a team to be aware of the importance of the fundamental elements of their service to act as a 'safeguard' when pressures are exerted. This is not a model of 'minimum care' but sets basic criteria or standards of agreed practice to which every patient or client can be entitled. Using these criteria as benchmarks to 'map' where your service compares is a good starting point and also opens debate about areas to develop. The 'Essence of Care' standards (DH, 2004), whilst designed for developing the fundamentals of nursing care, have been successfully utilised for whole-team development. Alternatively, standards and targets previously outlined may

- Shared sense of culture and organisation: aids cohesion
- Styles and approaches: positive 'can do'
- Whole-team working: supportive approaches
- Health and safety considerations: maintaining safety of patient and team care
- Therapeutic environment: preserving safe and effective care setting
- Staff and user perceptions: open and honest discussion
- Communication: effective and informed
- Responsibility and accountability: ensuring role support
- Information gathering and sharing: documenting, audit and review
- Organisational models and care delivery: helping maintain aims and vision of care

Figure 4.5 Organisational strategies for meeting demands

act as the catalyst to move the team and service forward if used with explicit visions and values that put the patient at the centre of the care process. The way forward is to foster a shared working relationship as discussed in the next section.

Shared working relationships

Teams rely on the interpersonal workings and dialogues of its members as much as, if not more than, just the professional skills and cooperation of a 'clinical team'. Like any 'family' there is potential for disharmony as well as support and trust. The way that such tensions are acknowledged and managed is a good indication of the mature working relationship of a team. This maturity is a prerequisite for excellence in care even if at times the team has to address some uncomfortable incidents and issues. Much work has been undertaken on effective group working and key elements are well recognised. Yet the reality in daily practice is the fact that individuals, teams and organisations are unaware, unfamiliar or do not have the time to reflect or embark on exploring the hidden talents within their teams or what constitutes an effective working team.

Case study 4.1 Interpersonal factors and team players

You are a newly qualified social worker and have been invited to the re-habilitation team's away day. As part of the away day you have been requested to participate in completing a personality inventory to see your preferred individual and team attributes and how these contribute to enabling you to become an effective team member.

For more information about interpersonal factors and team playing read on and compare your answers with the findings from the research in Figure 4.7.

According to Case study 4.1 it is evident that effective team working is dependent on seven key principles:

- Open communication
- Mutual support
- Sense of purpose
- Sense of direction
- Feelings of worth
- Being heard and valued

By exploring these key principles of effective team working it is fair to conclude that good teams do not happen by chance. Styles of leadership and facilitation play a key role along with hard work by individuals in pursuit of a collective responsibility for care (McCormack & Hopkins, 1994). There is inevitably a compromise between the needs and desires of the individual and the 'greater good'. Many teams deliberately focus on developing themselves through strategies of utilising group theories of performance. There are some classic models of group dynamics which continue to be of benefit for team understanding and development. A framework of group phases by Tuckman (1965) in Figure 4.6 outlines some well recognised (and often difficult) stages of development that a group may encounter. These can help a leader or facilitator to recognise where a group or team is in its development and facilitate successful progress towards effective performance

- Forming (group meets and introductions take place)
- Norming (rules and purposes are decided)
- Storming (barriers, conflicts and tensions occur)
- Performing (group addresses its task in a mature manner)
- Adjourning (group's task is completed)

Figure 4.6 Group phases to team development

Other well-known and helpful exercises use 'unfreezing; movement and refreezing' (Lewin, 1951) to describe these stages and help to focus on the required stages. French et al. (1985) suggest further movements to manage planned change and help team movement:

- Initial problem identification
- Obtaining information or data
- Problem diagnosis
- Action planning
- Implementation
- Follow-up and stabilisation
- Assessment of consequences
- Learning from the process

Whilst it is argued that change and its management is rarely so neat, linear and logical (Buchanan & Badham, 1999) there is usually merit in providing guidance for a team, particularly in its early stages of working. It can also allow a focus on the individual team member's contribution to a team in allowing each to consider their own styles of performance in the group and its implications for the group as a whole. This is further discussed in the next section.

Individual contributions to team working

All teams rely on a diverse range of roles being undertaken to support group development and functioning. These aid collaboration and closer working, promoting feedback, agreement and appropriate challenge strategies associated with learning organisations. These individual roles help to support the dynamic and complex whole of a structured functional team in systems thinking interdependence. Some of these roles may initially appear more attractive or desirable than others, but the reality is that groups or teams work well when there is a balance of roles in evidence. The following are well established in organisational theory and are proposed as key roles in team membership (Belbin, 2004). Again they can help the individual, the leader or facilitator and other team members to recognise where strengths lie, potential conflicts exist and where development opportunities are highlighted as in Figure 4.7.

Group roles: Consider your role as a team member and ask yourself: Which of the following do I primarily adopt?
Implementer? Organised and practical (possibly slow)
Shaper? Energetic. Challenges others to move forward (can be insensitive)
Completer/finisher? Reliable. Sees through to end (can worry/not trust)
Plant? Solves problems creatively. Original (can ignore detail/not communicate)
Monitor/evaluator? Thinks carefully. Sees big picture (may not inspire)
Specialist? Expert in key areas (may not have interest outside them)
Co-ordinator? Respected leader. Focused (can be controlling)
Team worker? Listener. Caring for others (may avoid decision-making)
Resourcer/investigator? Explores new ideas. Energetic (can lose interest)

Figure 4.7 Belbin's (2004) approaches to team development through role identification

According to Figure 4.7 it would be fair to argue that an effective team is generally made up of a combination of all the potential styles. However, this is rare, and for a team to move forward it is important that you are aware of these combinations in order to maximise the strengths, weaknesses, opportunities and threats that face the team in the future. A balanced team would have one coordinator or shaper to lead, a plant to stimulate ideas, a monitor/evaluator to maintain clarity and one or more of the other roles to make things happen (Belbin, 2004). Within the shared and clinical governance context it is no longer acceptable or indeed cost-effective to go it alone! Effective teams are an absolute requirement at all levels in order to promote excellence and this necessitates development and growth towards mature and effective working.

Apart from the obvious benefits of coherent and supportive group working towards achieving quality of care or excellence, there are essential rewards from effective group working that aid the individual's development and sense of well-being. Other than reviewing roles within groups, another approach is to consider the predominant approaches undertaken by group members both by the individual and other team members using statements like those offered in Figure 4.8.

- Proposing: a proactive transformational leadership strategy
- Seeking information: a careful, fully informed strategy
- Giving information: an authoritative strategy
- Summarising/building: a reflective, consolidatory strategy
- Encouraging: a facilitative, supportive strategy
- Gate keeping: a strategy based on control
- Harmonising: a smoothing, peacemaking strategy

Figure 4.8 Predominant approaches displayed in a team setting

These are considered to be essentially functional roles for the group if applied in a balanced way. Conversely, a 'dysfunctional group' will display less positive approaches, impeding the team working and can produce feelings of dissatisfaction in its members and affect retention and recruitment to its membership. Even well-functioning groups benefit from time away from actual care delivery in order to foster team building and effectiveness. This is often best undertaken by an external facilitator and may take the form of regular 'away days' or ongoing group supervision. The agenda needs to address both specific issues affecting group working as well as an opportunity away from every day pressures to raise individual issues or concerns in a supportive and non-threatening setting. To resolve the latter there are several practical steps that we suggest can be undertaken to assist shared working, as shown in Figure 4.9.

As a team develops and grows it is more likely that it will recognise its culture, how it relates to the wider context, what support it needs and how it facilitates its further development.

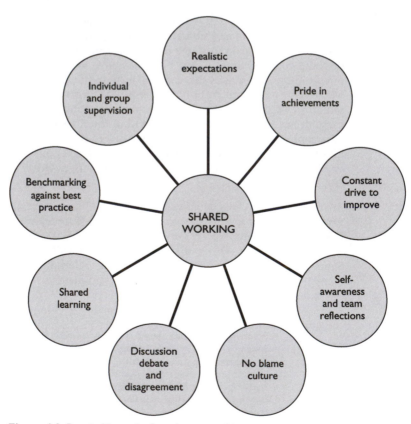

Figure 4.9 Practical issues in shared team working

Culture, context, facilitation and support

The team will benefit from examining its own operation and culture in order to determine if it is working, desirable and conducive to providing optimal care in its operation. Cultures of an organisation can vary considerably and can have a major impact on team working and care delivery (Figure 4.10).

- Power culture: a 'web' model; depends on a central power source to which everything refers
- Role culture: a 'temple' model; a bureaucracy depending on its pillars
- Task culture: a 'net' model; a matrix of groups formed for particular tasks
- Person culture: a 'cluster' model; the organisation exists only for the people in it. Control is difficult

Figure 4.10 Types of organisational culture (Handy, 1985:185)

Support and facilitation will be evident in both the internal and external working of the group. It is important that the styles and processes are congruent with the culture and context of the group as well as its aims and aspirations. Early work is often focused on addressing the culture of the group, its purpose and operation. Later activities are more likely to address change and change management and the role of leadership in transforming its operation and activities.

Transformation, transactional culture and emancipatory practice development

Many writers in the field of practice development have emphasised the need to move away from the technical aspects of change towards the idea of transformation of a culture and the 'emancipation' of the individual in order to better develop teams and practice and sustain improvements (Clark, 2000; Garbett & McCormack, 2002). This process of emancipatory practice development is considered by McCormack (2006) to have three components:

- Enlightenment
- Empowerment
- Emancipation.

These attributes encourage awareness, challenge and direction, and per-mission to change and, thus, transform. The importance of transformation, the role of leadership and the need for effective transaction has been well documented in changing and producing excellence in the ways care is given (Manley, 2000; McCormack & Garbett, 2003; McSherry & Warr, 2006). Many of these views I have brought together in the following way. Develop-ing the use of the prefix 'trans' as in the word '**trans**formation', i.e. 'across', to further aspects of the components of a service can usefully be viewed in the following model which incorporates much of the writings of authors on the subject. I have called this the 'transportation approach' to convey the fact that it moves something towards a goal or destination and takes the team with it. This allows the practice developer or team to remember the key issues in developing excellence in practice. The elements are expanded in Figure 4.11.

- **Transaction** involving *Emancipation* and *Empowerment*
- **Transcendence** involving *Vision, Experiment* and *Reflection*
- **Transition** involving the *Processes of Change* and *Change Management*
- **Transformation** involving *Positive Changes* and *Comparisons*
- **Translation** involving *Review, Evaluation* and *Acceptance*
- **Transmission** involving *Dissemination* and *Making Explicit*

Figure 4.11 The 'transportation' approach to practice development (after Mezirov, 1998; Ergestrom, 1987; Manley, 2000)

By taking each component in order it provides focus for the team's activities. Thus in the early stages the emphasis will be on encouraging all to feel part of the group and take active roles (transaction), whilst at the end of the process the direction will be on sharing the team's success and achievements with others (transmission). All other stages allow similar considerations.

Thus careful consideration of the attributes of a team and effective utilisation are the practice developer's key contribution to developing excellence. This is an explicit leadership role which will be considered in the next section.

Leadership and management

All of the above can only usefully be utilised within models of effective leadership and management. Key elements of the leadership role have been elicited in a range of research into the effective leadership of services, confirming the views of Adair (1983) and others. An effective leader utilises understanding, knowledge and skills, communication and empathy as well as good role modelling to bring out the best in the team members. He or she balances potentially conflicting needs, individual, task and group maintenance to take a team forward. This does not, however, negate the need for management of specific incidents and organisational requirements but operates these within a model of team leadership that values the facilitation of its members and the recognition of effective team performance within a philosophy of patient centredness. Reviewing the range of literature available as part of a larger ethnographic study into Practice Development Team approaches Dickson (2006) in Figure 4.12 reveals some essential ingredients for developing practice effectively and promoting excellence and these are offered as a guide for best practice in organisational change and developing a culture of excellence for teams to consider.

- Multidisciplinary team working
- A culture of lifelong learning
- Open communication
- Patient-focused services
- Staff empowerment
- Patient empowerment
- Education and training
- Continuous and rigorous evaluation and audit
- Research and development
- Sharing of vision and philosophy
- Innovative practice
- Dissemination of findings
- Flexible working
- Accountability
- Evidence-based practice
- Ownership of ideas

Figure 4.12 Ingredients for excellence in practice development taken from a review of the literature (Dickson, 2006)

Facilitation

All that has been discussed so far requires facilitation if it is to occur. This is a deliberate strategy to enable the process of practice development. The concept is not clearly defined (Simmons, 2004) but an acceptable view is considered to be that: 'facilitation is a goal orientated dynamic process in which participants work together in an atmosphere of genuine mutual respect in order to learn through critical reflection (Burrows, 1997). In another concept clarification Simmons (2004) identified five facilitation characteristics: critical thinking, shared decision-making, making things easier, leadership of change and equity. Thus direction can be given to creating an environment which facilitates development and change. Many techniques have been used to assist this process in addition to emancipatory practice development as previously discussed: action learning (Manley, 1999); supervisory and collaborative approaches such as critical companionship (Titchen, 2003) and reflection (Johns, 1996). These will often produce coherence and better understanding within the team and aid the role of the facilitator. All, however, are dependent on the desire and willingness to change at individual and organisational level previously outlined and creating a culture which enables individuals and groups to change. This responsibility, however, rests with the individual practitioners themselves (Grundy, 1982).

Conclusion

Organisations and services are complex and can be 'messy' (Schon, 1987) but are amenable to understanding, leadership and facilitative support. The key to change is the individual responsibility within a team approach that values individual cooperations but inculcates a shared understanding of the service and its effective delivery based on shared vision and values around patient centredness. As Fay (1987) observed, such a focus is enabled through: skilled facilitation within a philosophy of emancipatory change and the processes of enlightenment and empowerment.

Key points

- Consideration needs to be given to awareness, environment, leadership, empowerment and learning to foster a 'learning organisation'
- Services need to address the diversity of their demands in an equitable and equal manner
- Needs of both individuals and teams require consideration
- Organisational influences need to be considered and incorporated
- Effective teams have shared visions and values
- Clinical and shared governance are vital
- Teams are effective change agents
- Teams require leadership and facilitation
- Models exist for transforming care towards excellence

Further reading

Denton, J. (1998) *Organizational Learning and Effectiveness*. Routledge: London.
Garbett, R. (2002) The qualities and skills of practice developers. *Nursing Standard* 16:(50):33–6.
Redfern, S. Christian, S. (2003) Achieving change in health care practice. *Journal of Evaluation in Clinical Practice* 9(2): 225–38.
Senge, P. (1994) *The Fifth Discipline: The Art and Practice of the Learning Organization*. Doubleday Currency: New York.

Useful links

Department of Health at www.dh.gov.uk
National Institute for Health and Clinical Excellence at www.nice.org.uk
RCN Research and Development Co-ordinating Centre at www.rcn.org.uk/ research&development

References

Adair, J. (1983) *Effective Leadership*. Gower Press: London.
Belbin R.M. (2004) *Management Teams – Why they Succeed or Fail*, 2nd edn. Elsevier: Oxford.
Buchanan, D., Badham, R. (1999) *Power, Politics and Organisational Change*. Sage: London.

Burrows, D.E. (1997) Facilitation: a concept analysis. *Journal of Advanced Nursing* 25: 396–404.

Checkland, P. (1981) *Systems Thinking: Systems Practice*. Wiley: Chichester.

Clark, J.E. (2000) Action research. In: Cormack, D. (ed.) *The Research Process in Nursing*. Blackwell Science: Oxford.

Department of Health (2005) *Essence of Care. Benchmarks for Promoting Health*. DH: London.

Dickson, C.L. (2006) Practice development unit accreditation: literature review. PhD thesis in preparation: Bournemouth University.

Dixon, N. (1994) *The Organizational Learning Cycle. How We Can Learn Collectively*. McGraw-Hill: London.

Ergestrom, Y. (1987) *Learning by Expanding*. Orienta-consultit: Helsinki.

Fay, B. (1987) *Critical Social Science: Liberation and its Limits*. Polity Press: Oxford.

Finger, M., Brand, S.B. (1999) The concept of the 'learning organization' applied to the transformation of the public sector. In: Easterby Smith, M., Araujo, L., Burgoyne, J. (eds) *Organizational Learning and the Learning Organization*. Sage: London.

French, W.L., Bell, C.H. (1984) *Organization Development*. Prentice Hall: Inglewood Cliffs, NJ.

Gadamer, H.G. (1979) *Truth and the Method*. Sheed and Ward: London.

Garbett, R., McCormack, B. (2002) A concept analysis of practice development. *N T Research* 7(2): 87–99.

Grundy, S. (1982) Three modes of action research. *Curriculum Perspectives* 25:145–7.

Guardian (2006) Should you go public? 16 January.

Handy, C.B. (1985) *Understanding Organisations*, 3rd edn. Penguin: Harmondsworth.

Health Ombudsman (2005) *Annual Report*. Department of Health: London.

Hersey, P., Blanchard, K.H., Johnson, D. (2001) *Management of Organisational Behaviour: Leading Human Resources*, 8th edn. Prentice Hall: New Jersey.

Johns, C. (1996) Visualizing and realizing caring in practice through guided reflection. *Journal of Advanced Nursing* 24(6): 1135–43.

Lawless, J., Walsh, K. (2005) *Building Effective Engagement Techniques: a guide to bringing people together co-operatively to find sustainable solutions (version 2)*. Waikato Health Board: Hamilton, NZ.

Lewin, K. (1951) *Field Theory in Social Science*. Harper and Row: London.

Manley, K. (1999) Developing a culture for empowerment. *Nursing in Critical Care* 4(2): 57–8.

Manley, K. (2000) Practice development revisited: clarifying the concept. *Nursing in Critical Care* 5(4): 161–2.

Maslow, A.H. (1968) *Towards a Psychology of Being*, 2nd edn. Nostrand Reinhold: New York.

Maxwell, R. (1984) Quality assessment in health. *British Medical Journal* 288: 1470–2.

McCormack, B. (2006) Evidence based practice and the potential for transformation. *Journal of Nursing Research* 11: 89–94.

McCormack, B., Garbett, R. (2003) The characteristics, qualities and skills of practice developers. *Journal of Clinical Nursing* 12(3): 317–25.

McCormack, B., Hopkins, E. (1995) The development of clinical leadership through supported reflective practice. *Journal of Clinical Nursing* 4(3): 161–8.

McSherry, R., Pearce, P. (2002) *Clinical Governance. A guide to Implementation for Health Professionals*. Blackwell Publishing: Oxford.

McSherry, R., Warr, J. (2006) Practice development: confirming the existence of a knowledge and evidence base. *Practice Development in Healthcare* 5(2): 55–79.

Mezirov, J. (1991) *Transformative Dimensions of Adult Learning*. Jossey-Bass: San Francisco.

National Institute for Clinical Excellence (2001) *The Guideline Development Process-Information for National Collaborating Centres and Guideline Development Groups.* NICE: London.

Ovretveit, J.(1990) What is quality in health services? *Health Service Management* 86(3):132–3.

Page, S., Allsopp, D., Calsey, S. (1998) *The Practice Development Unit: An Experiment in Multi-Disciplinary Innovation.* Whurr: London.

Rycroft-Malone, J., Seers, K., Titchen, A., Harvey, G., Kitson, A., McCormack, B. (2004) What counts as evidence in evidence-based practice? *Journal of Advanced Nursing* 47(1): 81–90.

Schon, D.A. (1987) *Educating the Reflective Practitioner.* Jossey-Bass: New York.

Senge, P. (1994) *The Fifth Discipline Fieldbook: Strategies and Tools for Building a Learning Organization.* Doubleday: New York.

Simmons, M. (2004) Facilitation of practice development: a concept analysis. *Practice Development in Health Care* 3(1): 36–52.

Starey, N. (2003) *The Challenge For Primary Care.* Radcliffe Medical Press: Abingdon.

Tingle, J. (2007) An introduction to clinical negligence: nurses and the law. *British Journal of Nursing* 11(15): 1033–5.

Titchen, A. (2003) Critical Companionship Part 1. *Nursing Standard* 18(9): 33–40.

Tuckman, B.W. (1965) Developmental sequence in small groups. *Psychological Bulletin* 63: 38–99.

Watkins, K., Marsick, V. (1992) Building the learning organization: a new role for human resource developers. *Studies in Continuing Education* 14(2): 115–29.

5 Care standards and organisational accreditation schemes

Introduction

Organisations everywhere including the National Health Service and health and social care sectors of all types and sizes are expected, because of a combination of political, professional and public pressure, continually to improve their services, and measure themselves against world class standards for providers and users of the service. To assist and support this process many organisations are turning to Total Quality Management (TQM), or Continuous Quality Improvement (CQI) models and frameworks, despite the popularity and upsurge in the NHS of organisational accreditation schemes (OAS). Some NHS organisations are buying into OAS despite the fact that some providers and users of health and social care services are struggling to define and understand what organisational accreditation models/frameworks exist and what the relative merits and demerits are of engaging with them. This chapter aims to outline why and how organisational accreditation (OA) could be linked to excellence in practice. This will be achieved by dispelling some of the myths surrounding the various OAS and outline some of the potential realities in the form of strengths and weaknesses from engaging with OAS in the future.

Defining organisational accreditations schemes

Organisational accreditation is a very complex subject and a difficult term to define and conceptualise because it means different things to different people, organisations, professional bodies and accrediting authorities. Organisational accreditation is offered by numerous accrediting authorities covering general and specialist aspects of health and social care provision such as education, business and management, people management and professional registration to name but a few. Generally, Collins (1987:7) defines accreditation as 'to certify as meeting certain standards'. Perhaps this is why Chernay (1990) in Harvey (2004) suggests that

> accreditation assures the educational community, the general public, and other agencies or organisations that an institution or programme (a) has clearly defined and educationally appropriate objectives, (b) maintains conditions under which their achievement can reasonably be expected, (c) is in fact accomplishing them substantially, and (d) can be expected to continue to do so.

However, Naughton-Travers (2002:1), unlike Harvey (2004), airs a degree of caution when defining accreditation by referring to accreditation as:

> a statement to payers, consumers and the community that an organisation has complied with nationally recognised standards of best practice and quality. The accrediting bodies sometimes describe this as akin to the 'Good Housekeeping Seal of Approval'. The question, though, is whether the accreditors' national standards of quality are necessarily relevant to a particular organization in the markets it serves.

Taking the definitions of Collins (1987), Harvey (2004) and Naughton-Travers (2002) of OA into account it is clear to see why OA is difficult to define and conceptualise. This is because OA is often directly and indirectly linked to a multitude of organisational facets and standards which at times are difficult to untangle and decipher. At its most basic level OA

> involves the formal recognition of individuals, teams, organisations, services and/or programs in a particular profession, occupation or pursuit, in terms of specified objective standards relating to qualifications, competence and performance. Organisational accreditation occurs in the context of an identified organisational accreditation scheme designed to promote; accountability, communication, quality, standards, evidence and outcomes against given criteria throughout the team and or organisation. Organisational accreditation could apply to individual practitioners, to organisations which provide particular services, to specific service-providing programs, or to employers engaging practitioners in the area.
> (Adapted from the works of the National Mediation Conference (NMC) (2006))

Based on the review of the OA definitions offered by Collins (1987), Harvey (2004), Naughton-Travers (2002) and NMC (2006), whilst OA has different definitions, forms and functions, it generally has the following characteristics:

- It provides proof (or disproves) that a certain standard is being met. (The standard met can either be a minimum standard or a standard of excellence.)
- It involves a benchmarking assessment.
- The emphasis of OA is on accountability, quality, communication, evidence, performance and evaluation.
  (Adapted from the works of Campbell & Rozsnyai, 2002)

Despite highlighting what the term OA means, the challenge 'facing individual, teams and organisations is in selecting a suitable organisational accreditation framework that illustrates the efficiency and effectiveness of their practice(s) or service(s)' (McSherry et al., 2003:624).

The next section briefly highlights some of the existing OA models/frameworks that aspire to accredit quality improvements within the health and social care context.

Organisational accreditation schemes, models and frameworks

There are numerous organisational accreditation schemes (OAS) available for health and social care teams and organisations to work towards achieving accreditation. These range from government bodies or 'watchdogs'; for example, in England there are the Healthcare Commission (HC) and the Commission for Social Care Inspection (CSCI) (Adult Services) and Ofsted (Children Services). The responsibility of these organisations is to register, review and report on the standards and quality of care for a given health and social care setting. These organisations may also investigate complaints in standards of care and practice. In addition to these 'watchdogs' there are other numerous OAs which health and social care organisations access. These are aligned to measuring and accrediting different aspects of service provision such as:

- **People**   Investors in People (IiP). 'The Investors in People Standard is a business improvement tool designed to advance an organization's performance through its people' (IiP, 2006).
- **Management**   European Foundation for Quality Management (EFQM) Excellence Model. The EFQM Excellence Model is a practical tool that can be used in a number of different ways: 'as a tool for **Self-Assessment**; as a way to **Benchmark** with other organisations; as a guide to identify areas for **Improvement**; as the basis for a common **Vocabulary** and a way of thinking; as a **Structure** for the organisation's management system' (EFQM 2007).
- **Customer Service**   Charter Mark. Charter Mark (CM) 'is a powerful, easy to use tool to help everyone in the organisation focus on and improve customer service' (CM, 2007).
- **Multi-Professional Practice**   Practice Development Units (PDU) established to highlight multi-professional collaboration and partnership within a ward, department, service and organisation.

Despite the upsurge in the various OAS there are potential strengths and weaknesses from engaging with these in practice (Box 5.1).

Box 5.1 clearly highlights some of the potential merits and demerits for health and social care professionals and organisations who engage with OAS. It identifies the importance of raising awareness of what OAS are and how and why they may complement an individual, teams and organisations strive for excellence in care. Organisational accreditation schemes at best play an integral part in any quality improvement programme in highlighting to an accrediting body the evidence of how they have achieved a particular standard. They also encourage individuals, teams and organisations to focus on environmental, organisational, cultural and customer care issues and many other important factors which impact on achieving excellence. This is achieved through corporate and strategic visioning and action planning in order to bring about cultural change and improvements in the working environment. The limitation is that for this to occur requires financial

Box 5.1 Strengths and weaknesses of OAS in practice

Strengths

Offering a set of criteria for measuring a given aspect of care and/or service

Useful for visioning and values clarification along with corporate, strategic management goal setting and action planning

Useful self-assessment and benchmarking framework

Demonstrates an acquired level of quality and performance of practice to stakeholders

Focuses attention on continued professional development and lifelong learning

Useful if creating evidence libraries of how the team, organisation and service is collating, presenting and using information to inform and improve standards and practice within governance frameworks

Weaknesses

Raising awareness of what OAS are and how they may improve quality and performance requires financial investment

Time

Resource

Duplication of effort if going for multiple OAS

No one definitive OAS for health and social care

Note: This is not an exhaustive list and in no particular order of priority.

investment, resourcing and a commitment to release staff so they can innovate and change. The difficulty facing some health and social care professionals is understanding why and how OAS relate to standards of practice and what standards of practice are available to support the quest for excellence in care. The next section addresses the standards for better health (DH, 2004).

Standards for better health

This section is replicated with kind permission by the Healthcare Risk Report. The information is based upon the works of McSherry & Pearce (2004) titled *Healthcare Standards: A Critique of the Department of Health's National Standards for the NHS*.

The introduction of the Department of Health's *Standards for Better Health* (2004) can be attributed to a combination of several issues involving societal, political and professional factors. These include changes in health policy, rising patient/carer expectations, increased patient dependency, technology advances, demographic changes in society, changes in care delivery systems, lack of public confidence in the National Health Service (NHS), threat of litigation and demand for greater access to information (McSherry & Pearce, 2007).

Activity 5.1 Health and social care standards

What do you understand by the term health and social care standards? Why do you think these have been developed? What aspects of health and social care do you think these standards should cover?

Read on and then compare your responses with those in the feedback box at the end of this section.

The need for standards in care

The provision of accessible, equitable, high-quality care and services is difficult for the NHS to achieve. The ideal is a service that provides high-quality services delivered locally by well-trained, motivated people, that delivers the right care to the right individual in the right setting at the right time (McSherry & Pearce, 2007). This approach to service provision must be capable of demonstrating success in a meaningful way to patients, the public and healthcare organisations and ultimately the government. As emphasised in Chapter 1, in recent years a number of major clinical and corporate failures in the NHS have attracted adverse media coverage (Smith, 1998a). The Bristol Royal Infirmary Inquiry found the outcomes and care of children undergoing cardiac surgery there were suboptimal, while the Royal Liverpool Children's Inquiry found that at Alder Hey Children's Hospital body parts of children were removed and kept without the informed consent of parents. The public and government have realised that the NHS was not delivering what the public expected, including clinical outcomes comparable with other Western nations. So, what has happened to address service failures and indeed to fulfil the founding aspirational principles of the NHS?

The concept of performance management has been introduced and over the decades the NHS has been subjected to an ever-increasing number of targets and performance measures. A reductionist approach is evident and often what is measured is that which can be counted, such as waiting times in accident and emergency. We would suggest that this approach has been extended to the concept of 'inspection', in this instance referring to internal and external inspection and review to assure the government and the public that the NHS is delivering good quality outcomes.

NHS organisations are reviewed by a diverse range of inspectorates covering a broad spectrum of NHS activity. These inspecting organisations appear to work in splendid isolation, often examining similar areas from a slightly different perspective and on occasion reaching very different conclusions. These inconsistencies lead to confusion over the expectations of the inspectorates, placing ever-increasing demands on NHS organisations, which deploy disproportionate resources into achieving targets and preparing for inspection. The present government's NHS Plan (2000) promises investment and reform through modernisation. The NHS has undoubtedly been subjected to over-inspection with the emphasis on targets leading to low morale and demotivated staff. This point was highlighted in the Bristol Royal Infirmary Inquiry report and the recommendation made that 'the NHS should have national standards'. In response the Department of Health has attempted to produce national generic standards for the entire service.

Defining health and social care standards

Health and social care standards as referred to in the Bristol report are defined as a level which others accept as the baseline for good practice, the desired level of achievement (Schroder & Maibusch, 1984). Successive DH White Papers (1997; 1998) place emphasis on the importance of improving and assuring the quality of care, treatment and services through the principles of clinical governance. This is a major feature in guaranteeing quality to the public and the NHS; that clinical, managerial and educational practice is based on measurable evidence (McSherry & Haddock, 1999). Quality improvements have been placed at the forefront of the NHS agenda and clinical effectiveness is to be measured and evaluated against the proposed set of healthcare standards.

We would argue that there is a definite need for an integrated approach to the establishment of healthcare standards in the NHS. Organisational standards and accreditation schemes are essential for demonstrating acquired levels of excellence within any organisation. They provide excellent frameworks for promoting quality improvements, and as a result support organisations and professionals in making practice open and accountable. Our recent experiences of working with organisational standards, along with assessing levels of achieved practice, identify that they require organisational and managerial support, resources and financial backing.

Organisational standard measurement is an integral part of quality improvement. Practice areas need to provide evidence to the accrediting bodies to show how they have achieved a particular standard. Bodies such as the Healthcare Commission and the National Health Service Litigation Authority (NHSLA), through its Clinical Negligence Scheme for Trusts, require practice areas to demonstrate how they are providing effective quality care. The difficulties and challenges in the development of healthcare standards are in producing criteria against which they can be easily, consistently and uniformly assessed, which is perhaps a limitation for some existing healthcare standards and accrediting bodies. The way forward to resolving these and many other issues aligned to healthcare standards and accreditation is the production of a generic framework. The government is at least trying to address these issues by consulting with organisations and users of healthcare services on the proposed healthcare standards.

Describing the new health and social care standards

The document *Standards for Better Health: Healthcare Standards for Services under the NHS – a Consultation* (DH, 2004) was published in February 2004 for a three-month consultation period. The then secretary of state John Reid states in the foreword:

> These standards are not yet another batch of rules and regulations whose object is to tie clinicians into further procedures and targets (DH, 2004:).

The document has six key sections, of which section 3 details 24 core standards, and section 4 outlines ten developmental standards. These two sections are the key sections with which healthcare organisations and professionals should become familiar. The core standards attempt to set out clearly what patients can expect from the NHS. They do not seek to establish new standards but bring together the vast array of complex and confusing guidelines, measures and assessments. In contrast, developmental standards are not absolute measures but more broad-based, concerned with assessing progress made with implementation of the NHS Plan and other key NHS strategy documents. The challenge for the organisation is in ensuring that they implement and review the core alongside the developmental standards. The 24 core standards are set out within seven domains (Figure 5.1).

According to Figure 5.1 it would appear that the DH is attempting to provide an integrated approach towards governance. The similarities of the domains with the clinical and corporate governance framework are striking (McSherry & Pearce, 2002). But what is behind each of these domains needs further exploration.

Safety is defined as 'the design of health care processes, working practices and systematic activities to prevent or reduce risk of harm to patients'. There are five associated standards predominately centred on risk, risk management and learning from experience of the good and not so good. One standard is a developmental standard, about the introduction and enhancement of the systems and processes to monitor and respond to risks continuously.

The definition for clinical and cost effectiveness is that 'health care decisions are based on what appropriately assessed research evidence has shown provides an effective outcome for patients' individual needs'. There are two core

- Safety
- Clinical and cost effectiveness
- Governance
- Patient focus
- Accessible and responsive care
- Care environment and amenities
- Public health

Figure 5.1 Seven domains of healthcare standards

standards and one developmental standard. The emphasis is on ensuring that care and treatments are based on best available evidence and guidance.

The definition of governance is that 'all providers of health services have in place the managerial and clinical leadership and accountability, the organisational culture, and the systems and working practices to enable probity, quality assurance, quality improvement and patient safety to be central components of all routines, processes and activities'. This domain is the most comprehensive and includes seven core standards and three developmental standards. The emphasis is on integration of clinical and corporate governance frameworks into a holistic and integrated governance model.

Patient focus is defined as health care that 'is provided in partnership with patients, their carers and relatives and is designed around decisions which respect their diverse needs, preferences and choices'. The domain includes four core standards and two developmental standards. The central aims of these standards are ensuring equity, equal access to information, the maintenance of confidentiality, and the involvement of carers and patients in their care and treatment and the design/development of new services. By extension we would argue that all of the NHS must be patient-focused.

Accessible and responsive care is identified as patients receiving services as promptly as possible, having choice in access to services and treatments, and experiencing the minimum unnecessary delay at any stage of service delivery or the care pathway. The domain contains two core standards and one developmental standard reinforcing the need for healthcare organisations and services to focus their attention on ensuring access and equity of services. It is notable that the patient focus and accessible and responsive care domains go hand in hand and could easily be incorporated as one domain.

The care environment and amenities domain states that care should be 'provided in environments that promote patient and staff well-being and respect for patients' needs and preferences, in that they are designed for the effective and safe delivery of treatment, care or a specific function (such as catering or pharmacy), accord an appropriate degree of privacy, are well maintained and are cleaned to optimise health outcomes'. This domain includes one core standard and one developmental standard emphasising the need for organisations and individuals to actively consider safety, support, patient privacy and confidentiality. It could be argued that traditionally environmental factors have not been seen as a high priority but are fundamental to patient and staff well-being.

Public health is a new area for standard-setting in the NHS. Public health in this instance is defined as providing 'leadership, and collaborat[ing] with relevant local organisations and communities to ensure the design and delivery of programmes and services which promote, protect and improve the health of the population and reduce inequalities between different population groups and areas'. This is a highly topical and important domain because of changes in demography and society. Furthermore, this is an underdeveloped field of practice for many healthcare professionals to implement. The success of this domain depends on developing partnerships and cooperative strategies with other public and commercial enterprises. Primary care trusts should drive this domain forward.

Care standards

The Care Standards Act 2000, Health and Social Care (Community Health and Standards) Act 2003 and the Children Act 1986 are essential regulations to follow when running a care service, highly relevant to individuals, teams and organisations providing and purchasing in the care sectors. In brief, the Acts, according to the Commission for Social Care Inspection (CSCI) (2007), outline the specific types of service that must be registered and give the minister responsible for care services the power to set national minimum standards. The areas covered are registration and regulation of:

- children's homes
- independent hospitals
- independent clinics, care homes
- residential family centres
- independent medical agencies
- domiciliary care agencies
- fostering agencies, nurses agencies and voluntary adoption agencies.

The Care Standards Act 2000 contains comprehensive information concerning the different range and types of service along with issues pertaining to:

- **registration** – for example, how it is determined if someone is fit to be a provider
- **fees** – how much it costs to register as a provider
- **basic requirements** to run a service (SCIE, 2007).

In an attempt to encourage compliance with the various Acts and associated regulations, SCIE have produced national minimum standards for each type of service. These cover areas such as the following:

- care homes for older people
- care homes for adults
- domiciliary care (home care)
- nurse agencies
- adult placement services.

To identify all the important details contained in these minimum standards would constitute a book in itself. To provide insight into the importance of the Care Standards Act 2000 this section will focus on the Department of Health's *Care Homes For Older People: National Minimum Standards Care Home*

Regulation. The aim of these standards is to 'acknowledge the unique and complex needs of individuals, and the additional specific knowledge, skills and facilities needed in order for a care home to deliver an individually tailored and comprehensive service' (2003:viii).

To determine whether the above aims have been achieved following a stakeholder consultation, a series of national minimum standards for care homes for older people have been developed. These focus on:

- choice of home
- health and personal care
- daily life and social activities
- complaints and protection
- environment
- staffing
- management and administration.

Each of the above standards has a series of substandards with a desired outcome illustrating how the overall standard should be achieved (Box 5.2).

Box 5.2 illustrates a structured and systematic set of criteria designed to promote choice of home for the user and how this should be achieved in practice. Collectively the seven standards focus on the provision of quality care for both service users and staff working in the care home sector. The standards aim to ensure that the environment and personnel working within the care home are appropriate for ensuring and meeting the needs of older people. The emphasis in the standards is about ensuring that both the home and the staff are fit for purpose, and can provide a safe and homely environment from competent staff. This will be assessed:

Box 5.2 Care standards explored

Standard	**Substandards and desired outcomes**
Choice of home	**Information:** Prospective service users have the information they need to make an informed choice about where to live.
	Contract: Each service user has a written contract/statement of terms and conditions with the home.
	Needs assessment: No service user moves into the home without having had his/her needs assessed and been assured that these will be met.
	Meeting needs: Service users and their representatives know that the home they enter will meet their needs.
	Trial visits: Prospective service users and their relatives and friends have an opportunity to visit and assess the quality, facilities and suitability of the home.
	Intermediate care: Service users assessed and referred solely for intermediate care are helped to maximise their independence and return home.

inspectors will look for evidence that care homes meet assessed needs of service users and that individuals' changing needs continue to be met. The assessment and service user plan carried out in the care home should be based on the care management individual care plan and determination of registered nursing input (where relevant) produced by local social services and NHS staff where they are purchasing the service. The needs of privately funded service users should be assessed by the care home prior to offering a place (DH, 2003).

In reality the seven standards emphasise the need to 'maintain and promote independence wherever possible, through rehabilitation and community support' (DH, 2003:x). The challenge for any health and social care individual, team and organisation is working through the relative merits and demerits of engaging with and applying these standards in practice.

The standards versus existing systems

> ### Case study 5.1 The pros and cons surrounding national health and social care standards
>
> A junior member of a consultant team asks the senior consultant what the benefits are of having all these standards and targets when we are struggling to provide the basics.
>
> The senior consultant responds by stating that there are numerous pros and cons to having set standards. For more information read the remainder of this section.

There are several pros and cons that seem to surround the introduction of national health and social care standards for the NHS. The concept of a set of national standards that attempt to draw together the key components of the business of the NHS is essential, given the disparity and inequity of service that continue to exist within the NHS. NHS organisations and professionals welcome the introduction of a set of national standards providing they support professional practice and quality improvement and do not add further to the bureaucracy of existing systems of performance review. However, as the NHS is such a complex and multi-faceted organisation, is it really possible to introduce such a framework? Previous attempts have resulted in crude measures such as the NHS performance indicators and have led to a lack of confidence in the systems because they were meant to be supportive and proactive and not reactive and policing (McSherry & Pearce, 2002).

The greatest weakness of the documents is that the DH has written the standards, and the Healthcare Commission and Commission for Social Care Inspection has been asked to provide criteria to measure compliance. We would argue that the vision of the commissions/inspections is to reduce the burden of inspection on the NHS, and not to make it even more complex and demanding. To adopt this approach will require genuine collaboration between those operating and providing organisational accreditation schemes such as Investors in People (IiP) and the European Foundation for Quality Management (EFQM). Is this really possible?

A few years ago we saw the Commission for Health Inspection and Audit, the National Health Service Litigation Authority and others form the NHS Reviews Coordination Group that in 2002 produced a document entitled *Principles of Agreement* aiming to improve the efficiency of reviews of risk management. Yet each organisation continues to disregard the findings of each other and continues to examine common areas and issues from slightly different perspectives.

The challenge for some NHS organisations will be in applying these health and social care standards to existing practice, marrying existing standards of accreditation within the health and social care standards. Furthermore, will the Healthcare Commission and the Commission for Social Care Inspection be able to devise a robust set of criteria to assess these standards to measure essential developmental aspects of a service?

Applying the health and social care standards to an example of practice

For the health and social care standards to become an integral part of demonstrable healthcare quality and improvement it is fundamental that they become adopted and applied at all levels of the NHS. To this end a whole systems approach to healthcare governance needs to be developed (McSherry, 2004). Figure 5.2 attempts to show how the seven domains of the healthcare standards fit together and that they are interdependent on each other through the use of a whole systems approach to quality improvement.

This approach recognises the need for an integrated approach to healthcare governance, where through the development of interdependent relationships it is more likely to succeed. It can be applied to all NHS organisations as it represents the very core of its business, delivering high-quality patient-focused care locally. We would argue that this encourages clinical and non-clinical staff to harmonise efforts for the benefit of patients in a coordinated and efficient manner.

The healthcare standards and care standards illustrated in Figure 5.1 will only be effective through the adoption of a whole systems approach. A whole systems approach reinforces the concept of healthcare governance applicable within an organisational and individual level, and how the essential components of each concept can be applied and reviewed under the key domains of safety, clinical and cost effectiveness, governance, patient focus, accessible and responsive care, care environment and amenities, and public health. Whilst the above framework is associated with competency or performance-related issues at an organisational, department/directorate and team level

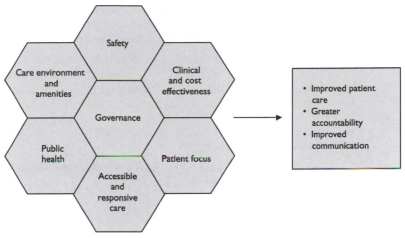

Figure 5.2 The interdependent relationship of health and social care standards
Adopted from McSherry & Pearce (2004).

the same could be used for promoting the NHS modernisation agenda. The key to successful modernisation through the health and social care standards is associated with the harmonising (or integration) of the clinical and non-clinical aspects of governance as is discussed in the next section.

Criteria for evaluating the standards

For successful implementation of the health and social care standards it is imperative that the Healthcare Commission and Commission for Social Care Inspection use their authority to encourage all inspectorates to unite. Unification of these various organisational accrediting bodies is imperative. The key disadvantage of organisational standards and accreditation within the NHS today is in the duplication of time, resources and support needed for individuals, teams and organisations in collecting, collating and providing evidence. Health and social care organisations seem to be pressurised not just in meeting the criteria for one award but for several at any one time (McSherry et al., 2003).

A critical review of the organisational and accreditation frameworks such as IiP, European Foundation for Quality Management (EFQM), CNST and Charter Mark has already revealed a set of the primary core themes in the publication of the Excellence in Practice Accreditation Scheme (EPAS) (McSherry et al., 2003). EPAS provides a robust framework supporting the clinical governance agenda because of its associations with the key components of clinical governance. There are many examples of organisational accreditation schemes but none of them capture the essence of clinical governance or evidence-based practice within a practice development framework. The uniqueness of the EPAS is in collectively addressing the key issues in developing, advancing and evaluating practice, which could easily be transferred and further developed to incorporate the non-clinical aspects of the integrated governance model and the healthcare standards.

The acid test for the health and social care standards and ultimately the Commission itself will be in demonstrating a reduction in the burden of inspection, by the use of intelligent information that ultimately leads to targeted and proportionate inspection.

Activity 5.2 Feedback

What do you understand by the term national healthcare standards? Why do you think these have been developed? What aspects of healthcare do you think these standards should cover?

Standards for Better Health and the Social Care Standards adopt a much broader approach to performance management taking into consideration the perspectives of the Department of Health, health and social care professionals and, more importantly, patients and carers providing a clear set of standards that all stakeholders involved with a given package or provision of care should be meeting. This new approach attempts to integrate the various health and social care structures and systems within an organisation using a whole systems approach.

Conclusion

Organisational accreditation schemes and standards for facilitating excellence in health and social care offer many opportunities and challenges in the future. Health and social care professionals, teams and organisations must avail themselves of these opportunities and work through the challenges if excellence in health and social care is to be realised.

Key points

- Organisations everywhere including the National Health Service and health and social care sectors of all types and sizes are expected, because of a combination of political, professional and public pressure, continually to improve their services and measure themselves against world class standards for providers and users of the service.
- Organisational accreditation (OA) is a very complex subject to conceptualise because it means different things to different people, organisations, professional bodies and accrediting authorities.
- There are numerous organisational accreditation schemes (OAS) available for health and social care teams and organisations to work towards achieving accreditation.

- Health and social care organisations are reviewed by a diverse range of inspectorates covering a broad spectrum of NHS activity. These inspecting organisations appear to work in splendid isolation, often examining similar areas from a slightly different perspective and on occasion reaching very different conclusions.
- Health and social care standards as alluded to in the Bristol report are being defined as a level which others accept as the baseline for good practice, the desired level of achievement.
- Organisational standards and accreditation schemes are essential for demonstrating acquired levels of excellence within any organisation. They provide excellent frameworks for promoting quality improvements, and as a result support organisations and professionals in making practice open and accountable.
- There are several pros and cons that seem to surround the introduction of national health and social care standards for the NHS.
- The key to successful modernisation through the health and social care standards is associated with the harmonising (or integration) of the clinical and non-clinical aspects of governance.

Useful links

Charter Mark http://www.cabinetoffice.gov.uk/chartermark/about/index.asp (accessed 13 August 2007).

Commission for Social Care Inspection http://www.csci.org.uk/ (accessed 13 August 2007).

Commission for Social Care Inspection – Professional: The website for social care professionals http://www.csci.org.uk/professional/default.aspx (accessed 13 August 2007).

European Foundation for Quality Management (EFQM) Excellence Model http://www.efqm.org/ (accessed 13 August 2007).

Healthcare Commission http://www.healthcarecommission.org.uk/homepage.cfm (accessed 13 August 2007).

Investors in People http://www.investorsinpeople.co.uk/Standard/Introducing/Pages/Home.aspx (accessed 13 August 2007).

References

Campbell, C. Rozsnyai, C. (2002) *Quality Assurance and the Development of Course Programmes*. Papers on Higher Education Regional University Network on Governance and Management of Higher Education in South East Europe Bucharest, UNESCO. Cited in Harvey, L. (2004) Accreditation. *Analytic Quality Glossary*, Quality Research International. http://www.qualityresearchinternational.com (accessed 13 August 2007).

Charter Mark (CM) (2007) *Charter Mark*. Cabinet Office: London. http://wwwcabinentoffice.go.uk/chartermark.aspx (accessed 22 November 2007).

Chernay, G. (1990) *Accreditation and the Role of the Council on Postsecondary Accreditation* (COPA) (Washington DC, COPA Cited in Harvey, L. (2004) Accreditation. *Analytic Quality Glossary*, Quality Research International. http://www.qualityresearchinternational.com (accessed 13 August 2007).

Collins, W. (1987) *Collins Universal English Dictionary*. Readers Union: Glasgow.

Department of Health (1997) *The New NHS: Modern, Dependable*. DH: London.

Department of Health (1998) *A First Class Service: Quality in the New NHS*. DH: London.

Department of Health (2000) *The NHS Plan: A Plan for Investment, a Plan for Reform*. DH: London.

Department of Health (2003) *Care Homes For Older People; National Minimum Standards Care Home Regulation*, 3rd edn. DH: London.

Department of Health (2004) *Standards for Better Health*. DH: London.

European Foundation for Quality Management (EFQM) (2007) *Excellence Model*. EFQM: Belgium. http://www.efqm.org/ (accessed 22 November 2007).

Harvey, L. (2004) Accreditation. *Analytic Quality Glossary*, Quality Research International. http://www.qualityresearchinternational.com (accessed 13 August 2007).

Investors in People (IiP) (2006) Business improvement through people. IiP: London. http://www.investorsinpeople.co.uk/Pages/Home.aspx (accessed 22 November 2007).

McSherry, R. (2004) Practice development and health care governance: a recipe for modernisation. *Journal of Nursing Management* 12: 1–10.

McSherry, R., Haddock, J. (1999) Evidence based health care: its place within clinical governance. *British Journal of Nursing* 8(2): 113–17.

McSherry, R., Pearce, P. (2002) *Clinical Governance: A Guide to Implementation for Healthcare Professionals*, 2nd edn. Blackwell Publishing: Oxford.

McSherry, R., Pearce, P. (2004) Healthcare standards: a critique of the Department of Health's national standards for the NHS. *Health Care Risk Report* 10(8): July/Aug.

McSherry, R., Kell, J., Mudd, D. (2003) Practice development: best practice using Excellence in Practice Accreditation Scheme. *British Journal of Nursing* 12(10): 623–9.

National Mediation Conference (2006) *National Mediator Accreditation System Draft Proposal for Public Consultation*. http://www.mediationconference.com.au/html/051117%20Accreditation%20Draft%20Proposal.doc (accessed 13 August 2007).

Naughton-Travers, P.J. (2002) Accreditation: necessary or optional? Four key questions help define its relevance to your organization (Cover Story). *Behavioral Health Management* http://www.allbusiness.com/health-care-social-assistance/262273–1.html (accessed 13 August 2007).

Schroeder, P.S., Mailbush, R.M. (1984) *Nursing Quality Assurance: A Unit Based Approach*. Aspen: Rochville, Maryland.

Smith, R. (1998) All changed, changed utterly: British medicine will be transformed by the Bristol Case. *British Medical Journal* 316: 1917–18.

Social Care Institute for Excellence (SCIE) (2007) *Practice Guide 09. Dignity in Care*. SCIE: London. http://www.scie.org.uk/publication/practiceguides/practiceguide09/index.asp (accessed 21 November 2007).

6 Practical approaches to developing excellence in care in oneself

Introduction

The previous chapters have emphasised the importance of cultural change and team working in developing excellence in practice. Much of the emphasis has been on the need to consider and develop strategic approaches utilising the expertise of team members within a whole system approach. This chapter places the focus on the individual practitioner and the ways in which 'practice expertise' can be developed by each group member through professional development models fostering the notion of each member being a practice developer within both individual professional responsibility and coordinated team approaches. To start this process we will consider some of the key issues.

Practical approaches to developing excellence in care for oneself

Within this section several practical ways of developing excellence in care for oneself is provided. The importance of focusing on self is important because without exploring our own strengths, weakness and areas for growth and development how can we share and learn this with others?

Codes of professional conduct and professional regulation

Each distinct profession has a duty to both the public and the professional bodies to provide safe and effective care within models of responsibility and accountability frequently embodied in codes of conduct. These give guidance on the expectations of the practitioner. The codes usually specify minimal professional knowledge, behaviour and attitudes, rather than optimal standards. Deficiencies are often identified through reference to these codes and become the province of disciplinary processes which support these guides. It is imperative that each practitioner abides by their code but it should remain merely a foundation for innovative, creative, evidence-based practice within the wider context of excellence in care. All codes, however, emphasise the importance of maintaining and developing the practitioner's capabilities and competence and the importance of continuing development.

Continuing professional development and lifelong learning

'Practice expertise' and 'expert practice' have become watchwords in professional development and practice development literature (Jasper, 1994; RCN, 2005). Allied to these concepts is the importance of continuing professional development and, more generally, lifelong learning. These emphasise the need to adapt and develop initial competence to meet increasingly complex demands of care and practice. They also suggest the need to keep abreast of (or ahead of) perpetually changing service delivery. Certain factors have been suggested (RCN, 2005) which define professionalism and act as enablers to practice expertise:

- **Reflective ability:** reflecting on practice in order to learn from experience, both good and not so good, to the furtherance of providing person/people-centred care.
- **Organisation of practice:** ensuring provision of person/people-centred care based on a robust systematic assessment, implementation and evaluation of care.
- **Interpersonal relationships:** understanding the best ways to work with professional colleagues and related professional groups.
- **Authority and autonomy:** having recognition from other professions and disciplines that the practitioner has the authority to make independent decisions and take actions in practice.
- **Recognition by others:** having professional recognition that the work and standards of practice are of a high standard of practice.

These provide a framework for considering one's knowledge, skills and attitudes as a professional and may indicate areas for development.

↻ Activity 6.1 Factors influencing professional practice

Consider your own practice against the above criteria and identify areas of strength and weakness.

How can you incorporate your considerations into a meaningful programme of development?

Compare your answers with the five attributes outlined below.

Further findings from the practice expertise report (RCN, 2005:12–14) have also proposed five attributes required for practice expertise:

1 **(Holistic) practice knowledge** which puts the patient or client at the centre of care and provides appropriate understanding for application in practice.
2 **Saliency** which identifies the most pertinent issues for the patient or client to then act upon.

3 **Knowing the patient/client** by emphasising the uniqueness and individuality of each person being cared for.
4 **Moral agency** through protection and respect of rights, and advocacy on behalf of the patient or client.
5 **Skilled knowledge** which includes all types or knowledge and skills to provide practice expertise.

It can be seen that consideration of both attributes and enablers as outlined above provide direction for continuing development and, when combined with appraisal and individual performance reviews, further support the team model of organisational excellence previously discussed. Thus it brings practice development and professional development together. Yet the reality in practice is in developing strategies for enhancing continuing professional development.

Strategies for enhancing continuing professional development (CPD)

Case study 6.1 Continuing professional development (importance of)

Within the model of continuing professional development (CPD), a wide variety of approaches have been found to be helpful in both identifying areas of strength and weakness and developing alternative and improved ways of practising.

For more information on developing a strategy for enhancing your CPD see the information outlined in Figure 6.1 and described briefly below.

Although all of the approaches outlined in Figure 6.1 can allow the focus on the individual and their practice, many benefit from application in a shared learning approach with the whole team (Miller et al., 2001).

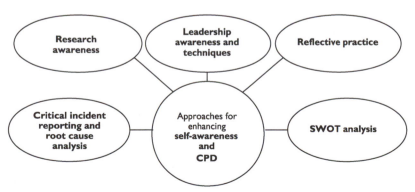

Figure 6.1 Approaches to enhancing self-awareness and continuing professional development

Leadership awareness and techniques

The importance of effective leadership in promoting excellence in care has been discussed in previous chapters. It is often overlooked, however, that effective practice developers may need specific awareness and techniques training in order to motivate a team effectively. Examples of leadership awareness tools and techniques are the NHS Leadership Qualities Frameworks and Myers Briggs Personality Type. Jasper & Jumaa (2005) in *Effective Healthcare Leadership* offer some excellent practical advice and guidance on developing a strategy for leaders which can be applied to the health and social care context. In addition, practice expertise requires the practitioner to embody clinical leadership in relation to the specific application of their professional role. Leadership training and ongoing development and support has been recognised as a powerful catalyst for change and service improvement at all levels of the organisation (McCormack & Hopkins, 1995). It can also have key benefits for strategic planning and service improvement strategies.

Reflective practice

Reflections on practice and becoming a reflective practitioner is now considered to be a key element of professional practice (Boud et al., 1985; Johns, 1995; Perry, 2000) and techniques for developing the skills have been incorporated into all levels of professional education and training. Inherent in this model is the ability to gain deeper understanding, consider alternatives and promote learning for the future. It incorporates an affective as well as cognitive appraisal and is linked closely to models of self-awareness (Rogers, 1961) and experiential learning (Boud et al., 1985). Use of reflective models and guided reflection are increasingly used in portfolio approaches to continuing professional development.

Strengths, weaknesses, opportunities, threats (SWOT) analysis

Analysis of strengths, weaknesses, opportunities and threats (SWOT) form the backbone of much managerial training and organisational management; the analysis of a situation, including one's practice and development. It provides a comprehensive and balanced appraisal of a chosen situation. It is a good starting point for exploring in depth, particularly at the commencement of a project or review of a role or practice. The work of Houben et al. (1999) and McSherry & Pearce (2007) demonstrate the effectiveness of using the SWOT analysis to support strategic management planning and individual personal development planning. Despite the effectiveness of SWOT analysis in bringing about change, Hill & Westbrook (1997:52) emphasise several areas for consideration as follows:

- the length of the lists
- no requirement to prioritise or weight the factors identified
- unclear and ambiguous words and phrases
- no resolution of conflicts
- no obligation to verify statements and opinions with data or analyses; a single level of analysis is all that is required
- no logical link with an implementation phase.

Taking the work of Houben et al. (1999), McSherry & Pearce (2007) and Hill & Westbrook (1997) into account it would be fair to conclude that the use of SWOT analysis, although important, has a tendency to be subjective because there is a lack of rigour and no inherent requirement to overcome any of the threats and/or weaknesses, let alone maintain the strengths and harness the opportunities.

Critical incident reporting and root cause analysis: ways of sharing, learning and improving practice

Developing a culture and working environment within an organisation that is conducive to facilitating excellence in health and social care requires introducing the key principals of honesty, openness and transparency. These principles and the ability to adhere to them are undoubtedly challenged during times of adverse events/incidents, complaints or reporting performance of individuals, teams and/or systems and processes within the organisation. Critical incident reporting (CIR) defined by the Intensive Care Society (ISC) (2006) *Standards for Critical Incident Reporting in Clinical Care* 'is any event or circumstance that caused or could have caused (referred to as a near miss) unplanned harm, suffering, loss or damage'. Critical incidents can occur in both health and social care contexts ranging from clinical, medication, patients' accidents/incidents, personnel incidents such as illness, abuse, violence, breaches in security, confidentiality and unethical practice. Documenting thoroughly prior to reporting the incident is the key to sharing and learning from the situation. As McSherry & Pearce (2007) and the ICS (2006) suggest, where possible incidents should not lead to disciplinary action but should be about sharing and learning from the experience of individuals, teams and users. The exception to this rule is where acts or omissions are malicious, criminal, or constitute gross or repeated misconduct. What is critical is the fact that all incidents whether near miss or not should be reported and managed according to the organisation's policies and procedures in line with governance standards. A simple eight-step guide to managing incidents provided by the ICS (2006) is outlined below:

1 Notification
2 Pre-investigation
3 Investigation
4 Analysis of investigation results

5 Conclusions and recommendations for action
6 Implementation of actions
7 Feedback to staff
8 Monitoring of actions

What is important for developing standards of excellence is the fact that evidence of sharing and learning from incidents occurs.

A root cause analysis (RCA) is defined as 'a structured investigation that aims to identify the true cause of a problem, and the actions necessary to eliminate it (Anderson & Fagerhaug, 2000). An RCA allows the problem or situation to be investigated by focusing on the What, Why and How. These are critical questions to address to prevent recurrence and to share a learning situation. The ICS (2006) and the NHS National Patient Safety Agency (NPSA) offer some excellent tools and frameworks for using and applying RCA in the workplace. The key to an RCA is involving all stakeholders to review the data and information in order to put systems and processes in place to avoid reoccurrence of the situation. A simple guide to RCA is:

• What happened?
• What should have happened?
• How did it happen?
• Why did it happen?
• What were the most proximate factors?
• Why did that happen?
• What systems and processes underlie this?

By following the above steps it is hoped that a sequence of the events leading up to the situation can be mapped and action plans and interventions put in place so that lessons can be shared and learned from the situation.

Research awareness: an important factor for evidence-based practice

Research awareness is vital to practising using an evidence base, yet there are no formal definitions identifying what it means and involves (Bjorkstrom et al., 2003; Jolley, 2002). The review of the evidence-based definitions and associated evidence (Banning, 2005; Camiah, 1997; French, 2005; Hundley et al., 2000; Jolley, 2002) illustrates a set of core themes outlining what research awareness means and involves. Research awareness is about knowing and understanding the importance of: patient participation, what research is, why we need research, what the research process means and involves, whether the research is appropriate for your patient, and what the barriers are to research being implemented in practice. By reviewing the works of Bjorkstrom et al. (2003), Camiah (1997), Jolley (2002), Kitson (2001), and Hundley et al. (2000) research awareness could be defined as 'a positive regard for research, through having the knowledge, skills, confidence and support to think critically, and to be able to appraise evidence, so that, this can be incorporated into everyday clinical practice'. To ensure the latter requires raising 'levels of research awareness amongst all health and social care professionals, which, according to Bjorkstrom et al. (2003) is crucial, and, surely, the first step towards evidence-based practice. The need for an ongoing debate surrounding the use of the term research awareness is central to understanding what constitutes evidence.

Maljanian (2000) argues that research within evidence-based practice centres on two themes: research utilisation and conduct. Research utilisation according to several definitions (Kessenich et al., 1997; Moore, 2001; Thompson, 1998) is regarded as a way of enhancing nurses' decision-making, because nurses require the knowledge, understanding, skills and confidence to be able to access, critically review, implement and evaluate evidence. Research utilisation is essentially about encouraging nurses to monitor their own practice, to determine if what they are doing is working well and, if not, to adapt their care plans as necessary with the support of best evidence (Abbott, 2001). The spin-offs from engaging in research awareness associated activity is the development of a professional knowledge base, enhanced self-esteem and a confident practitioner (Clarke & Procter, 1999). The challenge for many teams seeking to pursue and demonstrate excellence in care is how to develop a research awareness strategy. The sole purpose of a research awareness strategy is to focus on changing attitudes towards and understandings of research by demystifying the anxieties and myths held by nurses. The challenges facing higher education and NHS organisations are in developing strategies that sufficiently encapsulate the essence of research awareness (Hundley et al., 2000).

Developing a research awareness strategy

Studies by Fineout-Overholt et al. (2005), Hundley et al. (2000), Jolley (2002) and Wallin et al. (2003) show that the primary aim of a research awareness strategy should be directed at improving attitudes towards, understanding of, and increasing the confidence of nurses (indeed all healthcare professionals) to utilise and apply research. Based on a review of the works of Bjorkstrom et al. (2003), Camiah (1997), Jolley (2002), Kitson (2001), and Hundley et al. (2000), a possible framework for improving research awareness is outlined in Table 6.1.

Table 6.1 shows that raising levels of research awareness need not be a complicated process using technical terms or jargon. A successful research awareness strategy seems to be one based on simplifying the processes and terms used. By approaching research in this way, Camiah (1997) believes nurses may be encouraged to utilise and apply research findings in support of their practice. The contribution of Table 6.1 to the health and social care professions is in revealing the various systems and processes that collectively form the research awareness element and its relationship in promoting evidence-based practice. Upton & Upton (2005) and Bjorkstrom et al.'s

Table 6.1 A framework for improving research awareness

Content	Rationale
Drivers for evidence-based nursing	To provide information about societal, political and professional influences on the need to base practice on appropriate evidence
Brief history of nursing research	To outline key changes throughout UK nursing history which have had a major influence on the need to utilise and apply research in support of practice
The importance of patient participation, what research is	To demonstrate the importance patients' involvement plays in the development, implementation and evaluation of research and the impact of this on standards/quality
Why we need research	Essential for the generation and testing of new or existing knowledge
What the research process means and involves	To emphasise how and why research involves a series of steps/stages before it can inform decisions/actions in practice
Whether the research is appropriate for your patient	To demonstrate the importance of having and using skills of critical appraisals in reviewing and interpreting research findings and the potential impact on practice
What the are barriers to research being implemented in practice	To identify potential obstacles to research utilisation and application and how these may be resolved

(2003) studies confirm the need for health and social care professionals having background knowledge of the drivers for evidence-based practice, along with an overview of the historical events that have influenced the need to become research aware. This, according to Closs & Cheater (1999), is important in understanding the relative merits and demerits of engaging with and applying evidence in practice. Pickering & Thompson (2003) argue that health and social care professionals need to be made aware that the participation of patients, carers and care professionals in research is essential, if advances in care are to occur. Despite having this awareness, Carnwell (2001) believes many professionals and lay people continue to think that research is associated with advanced scientific activity, only undertaken by scientists or academics in controlled environments. Rycroft-Malone et al. (2004) and Fulbrook (2003) argue that research in and about care is essential in producing a discrete knowledge base for a given profession, and to improve the quality of care. However, Upton & Upton's (2005) research showed that the major problems facing some professionals is in 'defining what research is', and 'knowing how to apply it' in reality.

Reviewing the literature surrounding research and evidence within the context of nursing, for example, shows that the term 'nursing research' is highly overused to describe any kind of enquiry or information-seeking exercise. The International Council of Nurses' day on 'What is Nursing Research?' suggested that 'the scope of nursing research is as broad as the scope of nursing' (ICN, 1996:98). Furthermore, the ICN stated that:

> irrespective of the setting nursing research seeks to understand how nurses can positively influence factors that contribute to maximizing health and minimizing illness (1996:98).

A drawback of the ICN (1996) definition was its failure to acknowledge the interplay between research and evidence. Nolan & Behi make some progress in resolving this dilemma by stating that nursing research is 'a search for knowledge in a systematic and scientific fashion' (1995:111). Yet they omit to include the process. Long & Harrison (1996) overcome this problem by outlining the evidence-based process as a series of steps as follows: 1) identifying a problem or posing a research question, 2) seeking out best evidence, 3) appraising the evidence, 4) implementing the evidence, 5) evaluating the effectiveness of the evidence on the patient's outcome. The evidence-based process cited by Long & Harrison (1996), according to French (2005), encourages nurses to identify patients' needs or problems through information gathering skills. They then enter a critical appraisal phase, where they consider the research question along with the evidence available to answer the question. They do this by systematically reviewing and questioning the stages of the research process pertaining to a particular piece of evidence, that is its title and abstract, introduction/literature review, methods, results, discussions and recommendations and ask the following: 1) Is the research of interest? 2) Why was it done? 3) How was it performed? 4) What did it show? 5) What is the possible implication for your practice? 6) What next? – information only, uninteresting or support practice (Crombie, 1997). For registered nurses to engage in evidence-based activities requires education, training and support. Research awareness is about ensuring that nurses have the necessary skills, knowledge and understanding of research to practise evidence-based nursing or to undertake a research study. Furthermore, they need to be aware of the key conditions that promote or hinder this. Research awareness within the context of evidence-based practice as indicated by Bjorkstrom et al. (2003), Camiah (1997), Jolley (2002), Kitson (2001) and Hundley et al. (2000) is about nurses having an appreciation of the importance nursing research plays in generating evidence to support individual practices and decision-making.

Using and applying frameworks to develop oneself: the importance of seeking support networks

Owing to demanding workloads and reduced skill-mix practitioners may have limited time to seek out and build supporting infrastructures both internal and external to the organisation in order to support them to innovate and change (McSherry et al., 2003). Excellence in health and social care practice can only be achieved through building and fostering supportive frameworks within the practice setting (Pugh et al., 2005). Innovation and change is costly; it incurs costs such as time, money and resources, but more importantly staff require support (Hoben, 2007). Support can come in many ways, formally and informally, or direct and indirect (Table 6.2).

Table 6.2 Ways of supporting innovation and change

	Internal	External
Formal (direct)	Supervision – statutory or non-statutory	Professional support networks
	Mentorship	Conferences
	Preceptorship	Peer review and benchmarking
	Debriefing	
	Professional forums	Team building
	Action learning set	
	Critical companionships	
Informal (indirect)	Journal clubs	Shadowing
	Reflective groups	Networks

Note: This not an exhaustive list and is intended as a guide.

According to Table 6.2, there are various sources of internal and external help and support accessible to individual innovators, change agents or facilitators of change in order to enable them to advance and/or evaluate practice. If innovation and change in health and social care is to occur managers and leaders 'must understand the nature of support networks to improve patient [person/people-centred] care' (MacPhee, 2002:266). Managers and leaders must also become supportive and facilitative in empowering, enabling and encouraging individuals to access these support networks as part of the change process.

Support can be obtained from a variety of sources using a combination of resources both formal/direct and informal/indirect with internal or external sources such as the following.

Statutory and non-statutory supervision

Supervision can be viewed in two ways: statutory (as part of professional requirements) or non-statutory (as part of professional development or contract of employment). The value of supervision is the fact that it offers a formal arrangement that enables health and social care practitioners to discuss their work regularly with another experienced professional. Supervision involves reflecting on practice in order to learn from experience and improve confidence (Kohner, 1994). Supervision is described as a formal process of professional support and learning, enabling individual practitioners to develop knowledge and competence, assume responsibility for their own practice and enhance consumer protection and safety of care in complex situations. It is central to the process of learning and to the scope of professional practice and should be seen as a means of encouraging self-assessment and analytical and reflective skills (DH, 2003). Supervision can be obtained from professional peers internal or external to the organisation and may involve critical peer review and benchmarking dependent on the format of the supervision.

Critical companionships

Critical companionship is described as 'helping relationships based on trust, high challenge and high support, in which an experienced practitioner accompanies a less experienced practitioner on a learning journey. It is a means of enabling nurses [indeed all health and social care professionals] to acquire, experientially, the knowledge and skills required for patient care and its development' (Tichen & McGinley, 2003:115). Critical companionship is an ideal way of supporting the quest for excellence in health and social care through innovation and change because of the following reasons. Firstly, critical companionship is about fostering a culture of evidence-based, patient/person-centred care through facilitating individuals to learn with and from each other in a supportive non-threatening way. Secondly, excellence in health and social care can only be achieved by focusing on how individuals themselves act, respond and learn within given relationships with and between colleagues, patients, clients and other stakeholders. Thirdly, excellence in practice is ultimately influenced by the way individuals view and respond to their own professional knowledge base and how this is used to enhance their practice. Viewed collectively these factors indicate that critical companionship is an ideal method for promoting excellence in individual and organisational practice because it may be used to 'develop a strategy for working with practitioners who want to invest, generate, evaluate and develop service within their own practice' (Tichen & McGinely, 2003:130).

Action learning

Action learning is defined as 'a continuous process of learning and reflection, supported by colleagues, with an intention of getting things done' (McGill & Beaty, 1995). Action learning is ideal in supporting innovation and change and those charged with facilitating change because it focuses on bringing individuals together in small groups known as a 'learning set' where set members' ideas can be challenged in a supportive non-threatening environment with the support and guidance of a set facilitator. The learning set provides a balance of emotional and intellectual challenge 'through comradeship and insightful questioning which enables each member to act and learn effectively on three levels' (Bird, 2002:1). Firstly, to *present* the problem to be tackled; secondly, to *explore* what is being learned about oneself; and thirdly, the process of learning itself. These principles of action learning complement the quest for excellence in health and social care because primarily the role is about presenting, exploring and responding to challenge and change. What better way is there to achieve the latter than to share and work with individuals in a similar plight? In our experiences with action learning to date, action learning sets form a unique type of learning community or cohort because members come together in a voluntary and supportive way and form a contract to share, help and learn with and from each other.

Mentorship and preceptorship

Mentorship was described by Starcevich (2007) as a 'power free, two-way mutually beneficial relationship' and preceptorship was defined by Kaviani and Stillwell (2000:219) as involving 'contact with an experienced and competent role model and a means of building a supportive one-to-one teaching and learning relationship. This relationship tends to be short-term [and is aimed at] assisting the newly qualified practitioner or nursing student to adjust to the nursing role'.

Whilst acknowledging that 'mentor and mentorship' and 'preceptor and preceptorship' are different, they both offer excellent frameworks for supporting individuals in developing and evaluating practice. The challenge for innovators, change agents and facilitators of change is in deciphering the terms and using the appropriate framework in practice. Put simply a mentor, as described by Darling (1985:42), is a person who leads, guides and advises a person more junior in experience. Whilst a preceptor, unlike a mentor, according to Morrow (1984) cited in O'Mally et al. (2000:46) is a

> person, who teaches, counsels, inspires, serves as a role model, and supports the growth and development of an individual (the novice) for a fixed and limited amount of time with the specific purpose of socialising the novice into the new role.

What is certain about supporting individuals through a structured mentorship or preceptorship programme is that both have their strengths and shortcomings in facilitating learning in and from practice. Yet what is important to remember according to Ohrling & Hallberg (2000) and Ownes et al. (1999), is the fact that both approaches require investment, time, and active participation in the relationship, with a balanced responsibility for its success from both mentor/mentee and preceptor/preceptee, along with institutional and collegial support from managers, leaders and colleagues in practice.

Direct and indirect learning in and from practice

We use the phrase 'direct or indirect learning in and from practice' to capture a diverse range of support networks or initiatives that may enable an individual to benefit from working alongside colleagues or with other departments. This type of direct or indirect support offers fantastic opportunities for individuals to glean information, new knowledge, skills, competency and experience from the experts within the field. There are numerous ways of facilitating this through developing career pathways, succession-planning or through continuing professional development by offering shadowing, secondments or exchanges with different organisations, regionally, nationally and even internationally. A benefit from this type of approach to supporting learning may be the fact that the individual may not have to leave the organisation to attend formal education programmes or training. However, the drawback of this is that this type of approach to learning takes time, planning and the support of management to deal with any potential governance arrangements, such as arranging contracts for secondments and organising the secondment details and practical issues such as accommodation.

Networking: facilitating the sharing and dissemination of practice

There are numerous ways of supporting innovation and change through networking with colleagues both internal and external to an organisation. There may be internal professional development forums, where colleagues share and disseminate innovation and change, practice development and service improvements initiatives, evaluations of practice etc. This may occur once or twice a year. Similarly, journal and reflective clubs may be used, where small groups of colleagues meet regularly (monthly or bi-monthly) to share and disseminate ideas, opinions or findings from practice. Support networks may have a local, regional or national component with some more successful than others and with different organisational infrastructures (McSherry et al., 2003). The Developing Practice Network (DPN) (Integrated with FONS, in 2007 as part of the Developing Subscribers Area.) is a UK based network offering support to practice developers, innovators or facilitators of change for health and social care practitioners, which may support other networks in the future.

**⟳ Activity 6.2 The importance of active not inactive participation:
        the route to successful networking**

Read the following information presented by McSherry (2006) about the
importance of active not inactive participation associated with the DPN and
reflect upon your own involvement with networks.

Are you an active or inactive member?

We believe the following presented by McSherry (2006) could be paralleled
to all networks.

Firstly, the strength of any DPN (arguably any network) is its members,
who should possess the knowledge, understanding, skills and confidence to
facilitate and support colleagues who are engaged in innovation and change.
This major quality, integral to the practice development role of providing
facilitative support, is frequently acknowledged in practice development
and nursing literature. Yet, paradoxically, the support offered to practice
developers by organisations is often not reciprocated. So where do practice
developers obtain the support to regenerate and maintain their commitment, enthusiasm and passion to perform their role to an excellent standard?
For some practice developers it is through developing formal supervisions,
arrangements or action learning sets locally. For others who are less fortunate
in formal support, it is about trying to retrieve informal support with like-
minded colleagues and peers on the hop in corridors, following meetings
or as part of regional or national meetings provided by the DPN. Yet
again, paradoxically, during this period of change and uncertainty, due to
the demands placed on the role we have a tendency to stand firm in our
remit to provide support. Yet once again, paradoxically, as a consequence
of our dedication to the role we again exclude ourselves from obtaining
much needed support provided by local, regional and national networks.
This non-attendance and participative approach ironically impacts on the
strength of the networks.

Secondly, the paradoxes and reciprocity surrounding the term 'support' is
where the future survival of the DPN lies. The DPN is as only as good as
the active participation and support provided by its members in both
raising awareness about the benefits of the network and practice development activities to local stakeholders. Yet, because of the competing pressures
described above, if we do not participate in the activities of the network how
can the network survive? In light of the paradoxes and reciprocity surrounding the word 'support' I would like to personally thank those members who
are actively engaging with the network and urge others who are not, to do so.

Finally, during this unsettling period within the health and social care we
believe we need to harness the strength of the DPN network and other networks. This is essential so that we can collectively support members to rise to
the challenges facing them personally along with practice development as a

discipline Nationally by unifying its strength in demonstrating its importance in supporting innovation and change for the future. However, for us to do this efficiently and effectively requires active not passive participation (McSherry, 2006).

According to Activity 6.2 it would be reasonable to argue that support networks or groups must provide a balance between social, functional and psychological support for those who are facilitating and engaging in innovation and change to achieve the best results. If an individual, team or both are supported they too will be able to be supportive and facilitative to other colleagues. It is also worth remembering that the decision to develop, re-design, improve or evaluate care within any health and social care context will have needed organisational and management support in preparation of the bid to commence this important work or project. It is therefore inherent in such work that support from key stakeholders (both internal and external) will be provided within the organisation. The quest for excellence in care is primarily central to and dependent on developing:

- a shared vision and philosophy of care
- a common set of values, beliefs
- shared working relationships between all stakeholders
- collaboration
- communication
- commitment
- strategic planning
- goal setting
- action planning.

Networking or frameworks for sharing and disseminating information are the key to excellence, taking the time to invest in and build supportive networks using a variety and diverse range of internal and external sources such as those identified in this chapter is essential. Networking and communication are important on several accounts:

- to ensure that you have the help and support of colleagues, peers and departments to innovate and change
- for the sounding out and sharing of ideas
- to build a supportive network for the development of your own personal and professional development
- to ensure that you develop a robust system for the collaboration and communicating of innovation and change
- to encourage and engage staff so that they become acquainted and familiar with the innovation and change
- to establish a network for the sharing and spreading of advanced knowledge and evaluations regarding the innovation and change
- to ameliorate work-related stress, enhance self-esteem, efficacy and control.

Team building

Excellence in health and social care practice is dependent on effective team working which can only occur through knowing, valuing and rewarding the team and all its members. Taking the time out for getting to know the team and the individual players' strengths and areas for growth are essential ingredients for creating an innovative, dynamic, creative and supportive team. Investing in resourcing team-building activities, for example team away days, recreational and outward bound activities, whilst appearing expensive to resource in the short term can pay dividends in the future. Incorporated into any team activities could be the use of leadership qualities frameworks and learning style questionnaires, to name but a few, which could be used to elicit each individual's preferred learning styles, approaches and patterns to support innovation and change. The findings from the team's review can then be fed back to inform the sharing and allocation of roles and responsibilities for moving innovation and change forward along with forming the basis of any action plan for development. Team-building activities should be incorporated into any organisation's quest for excellence. As suggested by Team Technology (2007):

- A team is a group of people working towards a common goal.
- Team building is a process of enabling them to achieve that goal.
- If they are only a group, then traditional techniques can be a waste of time/money or even counter-productive.
- There may be better ways to resolve problems in groups: e.g. putting distance between people who don't get on or, if they are both willing, building some understanding of personality differences.

In summary, using and applying frameworks for developing oneself is undoubtedly a crucial factor in achieving excellence in healthcare. Focusing attention on raising awareness of the formal/informal or direct/indirect sources of support, whether this be internal or external, is imperative. This is because raising individual, team and organisational professional confidence through fostering a transformational culture, and creating a learning and working environment built on team working, collaboration and partnership, is a recipe for success. This, coupled with the principles of lifelong learning and continuing professional development, means that individuals, teams and the organisation have the potential to continuously improve knowledge, skills, competence and capability making them fit for practice. The challenge for any health and social care organisation is in demonstrating, through evaluation, that this occurs.

Evaluation: a major factor in demonstrating excellence in practice

Evaluation is undoubtedly a major facet in demonstrating excellence in health and social care. The reality in achieving this in practice is that demonstrating the impact, outcome or efficiency and effectiveness of an innovation, change, new role or service improvement remains both challenging and difficult to do. McCormack (2006:123) argues that

> the next era of advancements in practice development should focus on developing methodologies, testing out implementing strategies (methods) and adopting systematic approaches for evaluating processes and outcomes.

The way forward to enabling the utilisation of evaluation methods, systems, processes and outcomes is to identify what evaluation means along with some practical ways of engaging with the different methodologies.

Defining evaluation

Evaluation is defined by Clarke as

> making a judgement about the worth or value of something. This can apply in the case of the informal subjective assessments that are part of every day life, such as when we assess the aesthetic value of a work of art. It also refers to the formal, systematic evaluations undertaken by professional evaluators or researchers (2001:5).

Clarke's definition of evaluation is relevant to achieving excellence in health and social care because it focuses on the subjective and objective aspects associated with measuring the efficiency and effectiveness of a role or service. As suggested by the Health Service Executive South (2007:30) 'evaluation can differ in scale from a simple audit to a comprehensive evaluation of all aspects of a particular practice'. Sound evaluation is linked to measuring the aims, and objectives of a given innovation and change.

 Activity 6.3 Reflective question

The importance of evaluation in demonstrating the efficiency and effectiveness of innovation and change.

Write down what you think evaluation means and why it is or is not important in demonstrating excellence in health and social care practice.

Read on and compare your findings with those in the summary at the end of chapter.

According to Activity 6.3 it is important that innovators, change agents and facilitators of change familiarise themselves with the term and the processes associated with evaluation. Arguably evaluation is action-based with a distinctive and unique purpose. The purpose within the context of evaluating excellence in practice in health and social care involves a degree of logical complexity and it involves the checking and synthesis of a number of relevant facts, the determination that these are all relevant facts, and the combination of these facts with values, to arrive at an evaluative conclusion.

Put simply, evaluation within the context of demonstrating excellence in care

> is about undertaking a critical assessment, on as objective basis as possible, of the degree to which entire services or their component parts (e.g. diagnostic tests, treatments, caring procedures) fulfil stated gaols (St Legere et al., 1992, cited in Clarke, 2001:5).

These debates regarding evaluation are relevant to achieving excellence in health and social care because they provide practical advice and guidance on why and how to move forward with evaluating innovation and change in the future.

Conditions affecting evaluation of care

Based on the works of McCormack et al. (2006), McSherry & Bassett (2002) and McSherry & Warr (2006), the primary reasons for health and social care professionals not engaging in and with evaluation, whether it be at an individual, team or organisational level, seem to be associated with several fundamental reasons as follows:

Asking the evaluation questions

- Whether it works?
- Why it works?
- For whom it works?
- Under what circumstances it works?
- What has been learnt to make it work?
        (Health Service Executive South, 2007; Rycroft-Malone et al., 2004)

Selection difficulties

- How to access the information
- What is the best tool to use
- How to implement the tool
- The difficulty in choosing an indicator tool which meets the requirements of the service

Practice constraints

- Lack of time needed to complete and interpret the apparatus
- The difficulty of obtaining objectivity by the individuals using the measurement tools
- The costs which can be incurred by bringing in outside agencies to perform such reviews of practice

Interpretation difficulties

- What to do with the data when available
- Inability to implement the findings once the results are available

To develop an effective evaluation framework, innovators, change agents and facilitators of change need to be able to identify and resolve the potential internal and external conditions (obstacles) that are associated with measuring and evaluating excellence in care. The way forward is to develop an evaluation strategy built into the project, change or service improvement/evaluation.

Prioritising and establishing a strategy for evaluation

McCormack et al. (2006:125) suggest that 'practice development evaluation frameworks need to embrace the methodological principles of participation, collaboration and inclusivity'. To ensure the development of an evaluation strategy that is both efficient and effective in capturing these important elements within your innovation and change it might be worth asking the following practical questions.

- What do I mean by evaluation?
- What do I want to evaluate?
- Why should an evaluation be done?
- What support/resources are there available to aid the evaluation?
- How will I share and disseminate the findings of the evaluation?

In response to the questions above you may find that there are selection difficulties, practical constraints and/or organisational factors such as a lack of support/resources influencing what, how and why to evaluate the impact on patient outcome, services and/or performance. As part of an evaluation it is important to decide on what you are evaluating. For example, do you focus on *impact assessment*, that is determining the impact or changes that could be attributed or differentiated as a direct or indirect result of the innovation and change? Alternatively do you focus on *performance assessment*, that is reviewing the effectiveness of the change or project in helping the organisation achieve targets or standards laid down by government or detailed in given policies or standards like the National Service Frameworks? From our experience in practice development, it is counterproductive to leave evaluation out of the designing/planning stages of a new innovation/change in practice. Evaluation is both a process and a product making it inextricably important to the furtherance of achieving excellence in health and social care of practitioners and their employing organisation. The difficulties and challenges are how to prioritise and devise a strategy for evaluation.

A simple yet effective way to prioritising and devising a strategy for evaluation is to focus on the following:

- Types of evaluation
- Ensuring objectivity and consistency within evaluation
- Identifying the key components of evaluation

(McSherry & Mudd, 2005)

Devising an efficient and effective strategy to evaluate care should focus on identifying the type of evaluation to be undertaken – structure, process or outcome – ensuring objectivity and consistency in the process and methods employed, differentiating the key components to be evaluated, clinical outcomes, service improvement, individual performance etc. . . . and finally evaluation should contain a staged approach: design, implementation, mid-term review, completion, and sharing and dissemination. Some practical points to remember are:

- **Seek support:** you do not have to work in isolation; link with the local university or research and development department.
- **Search and review the literature:** do not be afraid to build on the works of others.
- **Contact** the people who have done it before locally, regionally and nationally and if necessary internationally.
- **Learn from experience** by talking and sharing with others who have contributed to the field.
- **Contribute:** be aware that you have something to share and disseminate, as part of your position, so networking and collaborating are essential.

Evaluation methodologies

Evaluation can be undertaken in a variety of ways: measuring and evaluating practice; clinical audit; patient satisfaction surveys; formal research such as randomised control trials; non-randomised studies; descriptive studies; action research; review of guidelines and guideline development; utilisation of leadership and management style assessment tools; and change models, to name but a few. To try to explain the advantages and disadvantages of the various approaches and methods of measuring and evaluating practice would be unwise. What is worth pointing out at this stage is that the key is to access and apply the best approaches or methods to suit the aspect of your role that you want to evaluate. For example, if an area of innovation and change involves a clinical team seeking the views of users for a given service, a patient satisfaction survey or research focus group could be used singly or combined. Essentially, evaluation is about utilising the appropriate measurement or evaluative templates at the right time.

Evaluation is undoubtedly a complex and challenging aspect for health and social care professionals to engage with and apply in practice. By focusing your attention on understanding the terminology we hope to demystify and clarify its usefulness.

- Evaluation is a generic term used to symbolise specific changes, meanings or happenings in practice. It indicates the relevance of a change, such as the introduction of new roles, through demonstrating the impact the change has had in terms of meeting its aims/goals, enhancing quality and providing value for money (efficiency and effectiveness).
- Evaluation is traditionally carried out at the end or close of the project, event or change.
- Evaluation should be a phased approach containing internal and external scrutiny.

More practical information on evaluation can be found in Box 6.1.

Box 6.1 Useful information on evaluation

For more information on evaluation review the following publications:

Health Service Executive South (2007) *A Strategy for Practice Development.* HSE, Nursing and Midwifery Planning Development Unit Southern Ireland.
McSherry, R., Mudd, D. (2005) Ways to evaluating the efficiency and effectiveness of the nurse/therapist consultant. In: McSherry, R., Johnson, S. *Demystifying the Nurse/ Therapist: A Foundation Text.* Nelson Thornes: Cheltenham.
McCormack, B., Dewar, B., Wright, J., Garbett, R., Harvey, G., Ballantine, K. (2006) *A realist synthesis of evidence relating to practice development.* Executive summary. NHS Quality Improvement Scotland and NHS Education for Scotland.

Conclusions

This chapter has discussed the importance of identifying and utilising 'practical approaches to developing excellence in care for oneself', which is an important factor in any individual's, team's and organisation's pursuit of excellence. Excellence will only occur if individuals, teams and organisations avail themselves of the hidden ingredients locked in many of the practical tools and templates provided in the chapter. Excellence in health and social care is costly and as a consequence individuals, teams and organisations need to invest time, money and resources into supporting individuals and they need to share and learn from and with each other. To this end team building and other related innovation and change activities are critical if excellence in practice is to flourish. Furthermore, excellence in practice can only be demonstrated by the evidence, which is why it is imperative that evaluation methodologies and methods are linked to innovation and change.

Key points

- Focusing on self is important; it is only through exploring one's own strengths, weaknesses and areas for growth and development that one learns and shares with others.
- A wide variety of approaches have been found to be helpful in both identifying areas of strength and weakness and developing alternative and improved ways of practising as part of continuing professional development and lifelong learning.
- Excellence in health and social care practice can only be achieved through building and fostering supportive frameworks within the practice setting.
- Evaluation is undoubtedly a major facet in demonstrating excellence in health and social care.
- The way forward to the utilisation of evaluation methods, systems, processes and outcomes is to highlight what evaluation means along with some practical ways of engaging with the different methodologies.
- Evaluation should contain a staged approach: design, implementation, mid-term review, completion, and sharing and dissemination.

Further reading

McCormack, B., Dewar, B., Wright, J., Garbett, R., Harvey, G., Ballantine, K. (2006) *A Realist Synthesis of Evidence Relating to Practice Development*. Executive Summary. NHS Quality Improvement Scotland and NHS Education for Scotland: Scotland.

Useful links

Bayley, H., Chambers, R., Donovan, C. (2004) *The Good Mentoring Toolkit For Healthcare*. Radcliffe Publishing: Oxford. http://books.google.com/books?id=5CUWBz7HrPcC& printsec=frontcover&vq=mentee&dq=preceptorship+and+mentorship+in+health+ and+social+care#PRA1-PA39,M1 (accessed 12 August 2007).

Myers Briggs Personality Type Questionnaire. http://www.teamtechnology.co.uk/tt/t-articl/mb-simpl.htm (accessed 10 August 2007).

NHS Leadership Qualities Frameworks (2006) http:// www.nhsleadershipqualities.nhs.uk/ (accessed 10 August 2007).

NHS National Patient Safety Agency. Root Cause Analysis Training from the NPSA; Root Cause Analysis Toolkit. http://www.npsa.nhs.uk/health/resources/ root_cause_analysis/conditions (accessed 10 August 2007).

References

Abbott, P. (2001) Implementing evidence-informed nursing. Cited in McSherry, R., Simmons, M., Abbott, P. (eds) (2001) *Evidence-Informed Nursing: A Guide for Clinical Nurses*. Routledge: London.

Anderson, B., Fagerhaug, T. (2000) *Root Cause Analysis: Simplified Tools and Techniques*. ASQ Quality Press: Milwaukee.

Banning, M. (2005) Conceptions of evidence, evidence-based medicine, evidence-based practice and their use in nursing: independent nurse prescribers' views. *Journal of Clinical Nursing* 14(4): 411–17.

Bird, L. (2002) *Action Learning Sets: the Case for Running them Online*. Worked Based Learning Unit, Coventry Business School: Coventry. http://www.shef.ac.uk/nlc2002/proceedings/paper/05.htm

Bjorkstrom, M.E., Johansson, I.S., Hamrin, E.K.L., Athlin, E.E. (2003) Swedish nursing students' attitudes to and awareness of research and development within nursing. *Journal of Advanced Nursing* 41(4): 393–402.

Boud, D., Keogh, R., Walker, D. (1985) *Reflection: Turning Experience into Learning*. Kogan Page: London.

Camiah, S. (1997) Utilization of nursing research in practice and application strategies to raise research awareness amongst nurse practitioners: a model for success. *Journal of Advanced Nursing* 26(6): 1193–202.

Clarke, A. (2001) Evaluation research in nursing and health care. *Nurse Researcher* 8(3): 4–14.

Clarke, C., Procter, S. (1999) Practice development: ambiguity in research and practice. *Journal of Advanced Nursing* 30(4): 975–82.

Closs, S.J., Cheater, F.M. (1999) Evidence for nursing practice: a clarification of the issues. *Journal of Advanced Nursing* 30(1): 10–17.

Crombie, I. (1997) *The Pocket Guide to Critical Appraisal*. BMJ Publishing: London.

Darling, L.A. (1985) 'Mentors' and 'mentoring'. *Journal of Nursing Administration* 15(3): 42–3.

Department of Health (2003) *Developing Key Roles for Nurses and Midwifes*. DH: London.

Fineout-Overholt, E., Levin, R.F., Mazurek Melnyk, B. (2005) Strategies for advancing evidence-based practice in clinical settings. *Journal of the New York State Nurses Association* Winter: 28–32.

French, B. (2005) The process of research use in nursing. *Journal of Advanced Nursing* 49(2): 125–34.

Fulbrook, P. (2003) The nature of evidence to inform critical care nursing practice. Unpublished PhD thesis: Bournemouth University, UK.

Health Service Executive South (2007) *A Strategy For Practice Development*. Nursing and Midwifery Planning and Development Unit, Health Service Executive: Kilkenny, Ireland.

Hill, T., Westbrook, R. (1997) SWOT analysis: it's time for a product recall. *Long Range Planning* 30(1): 46–52.

Hoben, V. (2007) Is practice development under threat? *Nursing Times* 103(24): 16–18.

Houben, G., Lenie, K., Vanhoof, K. (1999) A knowledge-based SWOT-analysis system as an instrument for strategic planning in small and medium sized enterprises. *Decision Support Systems* 26: 125–35.

Hundley, V., Milne, J., Leighton-Beck, L., Graham, W., Fitzmaurice, A. (2000) Raising research awareness among midwives and nurses: does it work? *Journal of Advanced Nursing* 31(1): 78–88.

Intensive Care Society (2006) *Standards for Critical Incident Reporting in Critical Care*. Council of the Intensive Care Society: London.

International Council of Nursing (1996) Nurses day feature: what is nursing research? *Nursing Journal of India* 5(8): 98–100.

Jasper, M.A. (1994) Expert: a discussion of the concept as used in nursing. *Journal of Advanced Nursing* 20(4): 769–76.

Jasper, M., Jumaa, M. (eds) (2005) *Effective Healthcare Leadership*. Blackwell Publishing: Oxford.

Johns, C. (1995) Framing learning through reflection within Carper's fundamental ways of knowing in nursing. *Journal of Advanced Nursing* 22(2): 226–34.

Jolley, S. (2002) Raising research awareness: a strategy for nurses. *Nursing Standard* 16(33): 33–9.

Kaviani, N., Stillwell, Y. (2000) An evaluative study of clinical preceptorship. *Nurse Education Today* 20(3): 218–26.

Kessenich, C.R., Guyatt, G.H., DiCenso, A. (1997) Teaching nursing students evidence-based nursing. *Nurse Educator* 22(6): 25–9.

Kitson, A.L. (2001) Approaches used to implement research findings into nursing practice: report of a study tour to Australia and New Zealand. *International Journal of Nursing Practice* 7(6): 392–405.

Kohner, N. (1994) *Clinical Supervision: An Executive Summary*. King's Fund: London.

Long, A., Harrison, S. (1996) Evidence-based decision-making. *Health Service Journal* 106(5486): 1–12.

MacPhee, M. (2002) The role of social support networks for rural hospital nurses: supporting and sustaining the rural work force. *Journal of Advanced Nursing* 32(5): 264–72.

Maljanian, R. (2000) Guest commentary. Supporting nurses in their quest for evidence-based practice: research utilization and conduct. *Outcomes Management for Nursing Practice* 4(4): 155–8.

McCormack, B. (2006) Strategies for implementation: the need to value complexity. *Practice Development in Health Care* 5(3): 121–3.

McCormack, B., Hopkins, E. (1995) The development of clinical leadership through supported reflective practice. *Journal of Clinical Nursing* 4:161–8.

McCormack, B., Dewar, B., Wright, J., Garbett, R., Harvey, G., Ballantine, K. (2006) *A Realist Synthesis of Evidence Relating to Practice Development*. Executive Summary. NHS Quality Improvement Scotland and NHS Education for Scotland: Edinburgh.

McGill, I., Beaty, L. (1995) *Action Learning A Guide for Professional, Management and Educational Development*. Kogan Page: London.

McSherry, R., Pearce, P. (2007) *Clinical Governance: A Guide to Implementation for Healthcare Professionals*, 2nd edn. Blackwell Publishing: London.

McSherry, R. (2006) The developing practice network: a period of transition and reform. *Practice Development in Health Care* 5(2): 115–16.

McSherry, R., Bassett, C. (eds) (2002) *Practice Development in the Clinical Setting: A Guide to Implementation*. Nelson Thornes: Cheltenham.

McSherry, R., Mudd, D. (2005) Ways to evaluating the efficiency and effectiveness of the nurse/therapist consultant. In: McSherry, R., Johnson, S. (eds) *Demystifying the Nurse/Therapist: A Foundation Text*. Nelson Thornes: Cheltenham.

McSherry, R., Warr, J. (2006) Practice development: confirming the existence of a knowledge and evidence base. *Practice Development in Health Care* 5(2): 55–79.

McSherry, R., Kell, J., Mudd, D. (2003) Practice development: best practice using Excellence in Practice Accreditation Scheme. *British Journal of Nursing* 12(10): 623–9.

Miller, C., Freeman, M., Ross, N. (2001) *Interprofessional Practice in Health and Social Care: Challenging the Shared Learning Agenda*. Arnold: London.

Moore, T. (2001) The relevance of research in nursing. Cited in Bassett, C. (ed.) (2001) *Implementing Research In The Clinical Setting*. Whurr Publishers: London.

Morrow, K.L. (1984) *Preceptorship in Nursing Staff Development*. Aspen: Rockville, Maryland.

Nolan, M., Behi, R. (1995) What is research? Some definitions and dilemmas. *British Journal of Nursing* 4(2): 111–15.

Ohrling, K., Hallberg, R.I. (2000) The meaning of preceptorship: nurses' lived experience of being a preceptor. *Journal of Advanced Nursing* 33(4): 530–40.

Ownes, H.B., Herrick, C.A., Kelley, J.A. (1999) A prearranged mentorship program: can it work long distance? *Journal of Professional Nursing* 14(2): 78–84.

Perry, M.A. (2000) Reflections on intuition and expertise. *Journal of Clinical Nursing* 9(1): 137–45.

Pickering, S., Thompson, J. (eds) (2003) *Clinical Governance and Best Value Meeting The Modernisation Agenda*. Churchill Livingstone: London.

Pugh, E., Lockey, M., McSherry, R., Mudd, D. (2005) Creating order out of chaos: towards excellence in practice. *Practice Development in Health Care* 4(3): 138–41.

Rogers, C.R. (1961) *On Becoming a Person*. Houghton Miffling: Boston.

Royal College of Nursing (2005) *Changing Patients' Worlds through Nursing Practice Expertise*. Royal College of Nursing research report 1998–2004. RCN: London.

Rycroft-Malone, J., Seers, K., Titchen, A., Harvey, G.B., Kitson, A., McCormack, B. (2004) What counts as evidence in evidence-based practice? *Journal of Advanced Nursing* 47(10): 81–90.

Starcevich, M. (2007) Coach, mentor: Is there a difference? http://www.coachingandmentoring.com/Articles/mentoring.html (accessed 12 August 2007).

Team Technology (2007) The basics of team building. http://www.teamtechnology.co.uk/tt/t-articl/tb-basic.htm (accessed 12 August 2007).

Thompson, D. (1998) Why evidence-based nursing. *Nursing Standard* 13(9): 58–9.

Titchen, A., McGinely, M. (2003) Facilitating practitioner research through critical companionship. *Nursing Times Research* 8(2): 115–31.

Upton, D., Upton, P. (2005) Nurses' attitudes to evidence-based practice: impact of a national policy. *British Journal of Nursing* 14(5): 284–8.

Wallin, L., Bostrom, A.M., Wikblad, K., Ewald, U. (2003) Sustainability in changing clinical practice promotes evidence-based nursing care. *Journal of Advanced Nursing* 41(5): 509–18.

7 The way forward to achieving excellence in care through practice development

Introduction

This chapter focuses on how practice development has the potential for offering a systematic framework for facilitating excellence in health and social care. This is followed by an overview of what to expect in the future series 'Excellence in practice development in health and social care'.

Practice development: a framework for facilitating excellence in health and social care

The drive for excellence in health and social care as detailed in Chapter 2 is based on a combination of political, professional and public demands. These demands are compounded by the rising contemporary issues, outlined in Chapter 3, which face individuals, teams and organisations continually to provide and improve the quality of care and services based on best evidence and standards of practice.

Achieving excellence in health and social care is undoubtedly both challenging and exciting for those individuals, teams and organisations that embark on the journey of innovation and change. Excellence, as detailed in Chapter 1 is, and will remain, a difficult concept to define and recognise in health and social care. This is because excellence and quality care/services are interchangeable and as such may vary depending on the perceptions, experiences, attitudes and behaviours of people, notwithstanding the organisational systems and processes required to gather and present the evidence against set standards or performance indicators. Furthermore, excellence, as described in Chapter 4, entails changing organisational cultures, contexts and working environments so that innovation and change become an integral part of the vision, values and philosophy held by individuals, teams and the organisation. To become 'world class', which, it could be argued, is an outward expression associated with the term 'excellence', the challenge for any health and social care individual, team and organisation is in developing, implementing and evaluating the systems and processes to achieve an acquired level of excellence. As identified in Chapter 5, demonstrating excellence is about seeking out and finding the relevant organisational accreditation scheme (OAS) with a given set of standards and frameworks that will support individuals, teams and organisations in working towards and achieving the symbol, status and recognition that accompanies the term 'excellence'. That is not to say that excellence can only be demonstrated through acquiring OAS, but perhaps through focusing on other mechanisms and ways of sharing and disseminating best practice developed by the individual, teams and organisations. For individuals, teams and organisations in health and social care to pursue excellence in care they need to familiarise themselves and engage with the essential recipes and ingredients for success.

Practice development defined is as a

> continuous process of improvement towards increased effectiveness in person-centered care, through the enabling of nurses and health care teams to transform the culture and context of care. It is enabled and supported by facilitators committed to a systematic, rigorous and continuous process of emancipatory change (McCormack et al., 1999:258).

Practice development is ideal for supporting excellence through innovation and change by offering a continuous systematic framework/process for facilitating the advancement and evaluation of individual, team and organisational practice(s). Practice development is about ensuring that person/patient centredness is at the heart of all innovation and change. This is because user involvement in care delivery and evaluation is imperative in order to bring about continuous quality and service improvements within the context of governance principles. By focusing on what practice development is and is not, it is possible to illustrate how individuals, teams and organisations could embrace the underpinning philosophies, principles, purposes, methodologies, tools and techniques to promote and demonstrate excellence in health and social care practice. In brief, this introductory text presents some of the key practical steps and actions to be taken in order for individuals, teams and organisations to embark on the excellence journey. The start of the journey should focus on raising awareness and knowledge surrounding the areas described in Figure 7.1.

Figure 7.1 presents a simple yet effective framework for individuals, teams and organisations to apply before embarking on the journey of excellence. Firstly, it is critical to unlock the potential of what practice development is and is not, and how practice development can support an organisation through targeted facilitation in developing a culture and context which supports innovation and change. Secondly, raising awareness of the political, professional and public demands for quality care and services is imperative. Thirdly, focusing on the contemporary issues that may directly or indirectly influence the pursuit of excellence is important in corporate and strategic development and action planning. It is necessary to view what is on the horizon. Fourthly, it is imperative to encourage, enlighten and engage individuals, teams and organisations to embrace a changing organisational culture and working environment. This is because change may be necessary to achieve the desired standards of practice. Fifthly, seeking out and finding

Figure 7.1 Commencing the journey towards excellence in care

the relevant standards and organisational accreditation schemes can be challenging, time-consuming and resource-intensive. It is important to find a scheme that meets individual, team and organisational needs. It is possible to gain approval and recognition through other methods, such as awards. Finally, investment in people is the main ingredient for success. This can be done by offering practical approaches to developing excellence in care for individuals. Supporting individuals before, during and after a period of change is crucial.

Case study 7.1 Excellence in practice: myth or reality?

As a health and social care professional you have been approached by your manager to lead the team in the quest for excellence in care. How would you go about demonstrating this in reality?

Excellence in care is dependent on developing robust communication, sharing and dissemination strategies at a corporate, strategic, management and operational level with action plans that are supportive, facilitative and inclusive of all staff. To learn more about the above read the remainder of the chapter.

Case study 7.1 highlights that excellence in care requires individuals, teams and the organisation to work towards developing a shared philosophy which focuses on three key areas (Figure 7.2).

Figure 7.2 illustrates how excellence in care is associated with developing and sharing a philosophy, vision, values and beliefs which harness a goal of trying continually to improve the care and services offered at an individual, team and organisational level. It is about creating an organisational culture and working environment in which care can flourish. Evaluation plays an

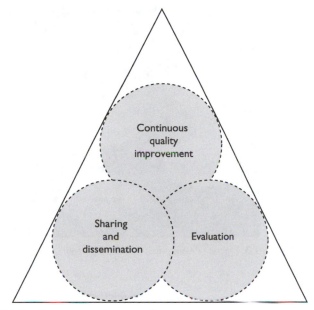

Figure 7.2 Excellence in care: key areas for success

important part in achieving the goals through devising and using different methodologies to attain the evidence to illustrate the standards of care provided. Furthermore, excellence is about sharing and disseminating successes and failures so that continued professional development and lifelong learning become the foundation of the learning organisation. Practice development is instrumental in promoting innovation, and facilitating change; it supports the creation of a culture and context that endorses person/patient/client/user-centred care. This is achieved by harnessing the key features outlined in Figure 7.3.

Figure 7.3 shows how practice development facilitates person-centred care through encouraging collaboration, partnership working, teamwork and building, accessing best evidence, devising methodologies and methods for evaluating care, along with supporting sharing and disseminating practice. By facilitating the above it is hoped that excellence in care will result.

Excellence in care: what to expect in the future

So what can you expect from the remaining books in the series? The series aims to focus on several important factors that collectively impact on individuals, teams and organisations, to work towards exploring what excellence in care means and involves. This will be achieved by focusing on the key dimensions outlined in Figure 7.4.

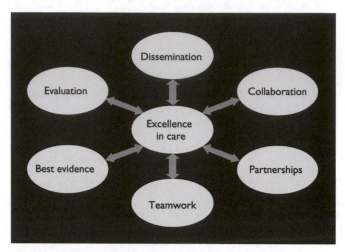

Figure 7.3 Practice development facilitating people-centred care

Figure 7.4 illustrates how practice development offers a powerful systematic framework for facilitating excellence in health and social care. Six core dimensions seem to influence excellence in health and social care.

Working in organisations

Working in organisations concerns exploring the initiatives under the policy outlined in *Improving Working Lives* and concentrates on team development, communication and the sharing of information. It concerns creating a working environment and culture upon which excellence can flourish.

Collaborative working

Collaborative working focuses on multi-professional working and development as the main issue for achievement of quality improvement.

User-focused care

The main theme of the modernisation and reforming agenda is encouraging user participation and representation so that users' views and feedback are both directly and indirectly incorporated into the development of practice. This theme focuses on the standards to be reached to achieve this in practice.

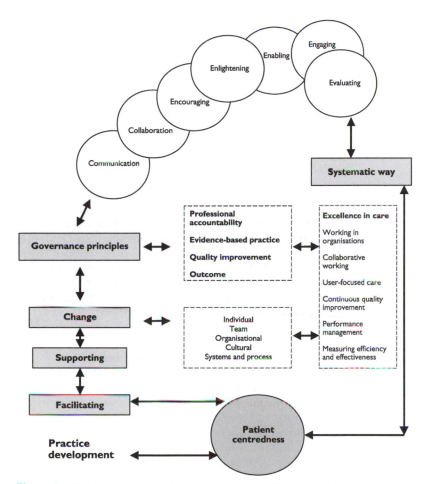

Figure 7.4 Practice development: a framework for excellence in practice

Continuous quality improvements

Within all quality improvement systems that have been introduced into the health service over the past 12 years the inclusion of improving the quality of care has always been an issue. Can the individual and the team incorporate the concept of quality issues in everything they do? This standard aims to make quality part of everyday working practice.

Performance management

To manage effectively is to improve performance and user satisfaction. This key component should concentrate on how this can be achieved in practice.

Measuring efficiency and effectiveness

To demonstrate efficiency and effectiveness in practice is to show how the systems can be measured and audited to illustrate developments and improvements in practice.

The challenge for individuals, teams and the organisation is in exploring the potential value that practice development offers in facilitating and supporting excellence in care. The excellence in care framework according to Pugh et al. (2005) and Hoban (2007) offers some new and exciting ways for innovating and changing practice.

> The excellence in practice framework has allowed the team to be more effective than the sum of its individual parts. Prioritization and rationalization of work has occurred and a common philosophy and vision has been established. Team and individual annual plans and objectives have been set. Duplication of effort has been avoided with individuals having delegated responsibility for specific objectives. An organic non-hierarchical management structure has evolved with a rotational team leader, individual delegated responsibilities and an understanding that each team member is of equal value (Pugh et al., 2005:141).

So what can you expect in the remainder of the series?

The series aims to build on Book 1 by offering practical advice and guidance surrounding the pursuits of excellence by targeting the specific core dimensions that surround excellence in practice. For example: working in organisations, continuous quality improvement and efficiency and effectiveness.

Working in organisations

The theme 'working in organisations' explores key issues and factors which influence the workings of an organisation and how these may be addressed through collaborative working and user-focused care. The theme explores areas such as working in organisations, focusing attention on: shared visioning through team-working and personal development; management and leadership development and styles; and how adopting a whole systems approach to viewing organisational change influences innovation and change. Within the term 'collaborative working' the importance of multi-professional working, team development, integrated team-working and how these factors promote or inhibit collaborative working will be discussed. User-focused care looks at the opportunities and challenges surrounding the meaning of 'user involvement' and how to achieve this in reality. Ethical and governance issues pertaining to user involvement, ways of engaging users, and the importance of maintaining equity and equality will be offered.

Continuous quality improvement

The theme 'continuous quality improvement' looks at how, within all quality improvement systems that have been introduced into health and social care, the inclusion of improving quality of care has always been of concern. Within this theme practical ways of incorporating continuous quality at an individual, team and organisational level will be provided along with detailing how continuous quality improvement is relevant to excellence in practice. Several practical ways of demonstrating excellence in practice through benchmarking, audit, research and development, practice development and service improvement will be provided. Finally, managing and demonstrating performance will be debated by outlining what performance management is and the associated systems and processes associated with demonstrating performance in practice.

Efficiency and effectiveness

The theme 'efficiency and effectiveness' focuses on demonstrating how excellence in practice explains how efficient and effective individuals, teams and organisations are achieving desired outcomes of care and whether these provide value for money. To demonstrate efficiency and effectiveness it is important to define the terms 'efficiency' and 'effectiveness' by outlining what the terms involve in practice. The various systems and processes required for achieving efficiency and effectiveness are required along with understanding the whys and hows of measuring outcomes in practice. Finally, an overview of the systems supporting and resourcing innovation and change in practice will be detailed.

Collectively the series of books will provide a detailed compendium of tools, techniques and templates to support the individual, team and organisation in achieving excellence in practice.

Conclusion

Excellence in care is challenging but achievable. Focusing on the hidden ingredients and recipes held by practice development offers individuals, teams and organisations new ways and insights into innovating and changing care and services for the future.

References

Hoban, V. (2007) Is practice development under threat? *Nursing Times* 103(24): 16–18.

McCormack, B., Manley, K., Kitson, A., Titchen, A., Harvey, G. (1999) Towards practice development – a vision in reality or reality without vision? *Journal of Nursing Management* 7(5): 255–64.

Pugh, E., Lockey, M., McSherry, R., Mudd, D. (2005) Creating order out of chaos: towards excellence in practice. *Practice Development in Health Care* 4(3): 138–41.

We wish you well on your journey for the pursuit of excellence in care.

Good luck !

Rob McSherry
Jerry Warr

Series Editors

Index

accessible care
domain of healthcare, 85–6
accountability
health and social care
professionals, 40
accreditation
challenges of, 22
practice development, 22–4
achievement
shared working, 72
action learning, 105–6
acute beds
maximising use of, 36
adult placement services, 87
adults
care homes, 87
agent of change
requirement for practice
development, 12
alcohol related problems, 39
Alder Hey Children's Hospital
body parts scandal, 83
amenities
domain of healthcare, 85–6
approachability
requirement for practice
development, 12
audit, 66
Australia
practice development in, 3
authority
factor defining
professionalism, 96
autonomy
factor defining
professionalism, 96
available resources
for achieving excellence, 47

basic requirements
care providers, 87
bed occupancy, 41
benchmarking, 26

shared working, 72
best practice
fostering of, 52
Bristol Royal Infirmary
Inquiry, 83
Building Effective Engagement
Techniques (BEET) model,
62
Burford Unit, 23

care
emphasis on, 52
evaluation of, 110–2
need for standards in, 83–4
organisational
considerations for, 61–62
care delivery
organisational change, 36
care environment
domain of healthcare, 85–6
care homes
adults, 87
choice of, 88
older people, 87
Care Homes For Older People:
National Minimum
Standards Care Home
Regulation, 87–8
care providers
basic requirements, 87
fees for registration, 87
registration, 87
care standards
choice of home, 88
new, 87–9
Care Standards Act, 2000
main provisions of, 87
care technology
advances in, 41–2
carer expectations, 1
change
comparative models for,
63–64

characteristics
required for practice
development, 12–3
Charter Mark (CM), 23, 81, 91
Children Act, 1986
main provisions of, 87
choice of home
care standards, 88
chronic obstructive pulmonary
disease
patient management, 36
Citizens' Charter, The (1993),
32, 37
Climbé, Victoria, 39
clinical competence, 66
clinical effectiveness
domain of healthcare, 85–6
clinical governance, 35, 66
clinical negligence
compensation, 42
Clinical Negligence Scheme
for Trusts (CNST), 23, 84,
91
Clinical Pathways, 63
clinical success and failures
publication of, 39
cluster model
person culture, 73
Cochrane Library, 39
codes of professional conduct,
95
collaborative working, 124,
126
definition of, 25
promoting, 55
Commission for Health
Inspection and Audit,
90
Commission for Patient and
Public Involvement, 32
Commission for Social Care
Inspection (CSCI), 87,
89–90

commitment
  requirement for practice
    development, 12
communication
  required for practice
    development, 9
community beds
  maximising use of, 36
compensation
  clinical negligence, 42
complaints
  increase in, 42
continuing professional
    development (CPD), 41,
    96
  enhancing, 97
continuous innovation
  for achieving excellence, 47
Continuous Quality
    Improvement (CQI), 63,
    79, 127
  definition of, 25
  key area for achieving
    excellence, 123
contract
  care homes, 88
contract of employment
  health and social care
    professionals, 40–1
coronary heart disease
  reduction in deaths due to,
    38
corporate governance, 65–6
cost effectiveness
  domain of healthcare, 85–6
critical companionships, 105
critical incident reporting
    (CIR), 99–100
critical social theory
  practice development, 10–1

debate
  shared working, 72
demands
  organisation strategies for
    meeting, 68
demographic changes, 1, 38–9
Department of Health website,
    39
dependency, 1
Developing Practice Network
    (DPN), 107–8

Developing Subscribers Area
    FONs, 57
diabetes
  increased prevalence of, 38
  patient management, 36
direct learning from practice,
    107
disagreement
  shared working, 72
discharge planning, 41
discussion
  shared working, 72
dissemination
  key area for achieving
    excellence, 123
diversity
  need for, 61
Doctor Foster website, 39
domiciliary care, 87
drivers for excellence, 33
drug related problems, 39
duty of care, 66
  health and social care
    professionals, 40

education, 66
Effective Healthcare
    Leadership, 98
effectiveness, 127
  measuring, 25, 126
efficiency, 127
  measuring, 25, 126
  types of, 50
emancipatory practice
    development, 73–74
empowerment
  emancipatory practice
    development, 73
encouragement
  requirement for practice
    development, 12
enlightenment
  emancipatory practice
    development, 73
equality of services
  need for, 61
equity
  need for, 61
'Essence of Care' standards, 68
European Foundation for
    Quality Management
    (EFQM), 23, 81, 90–1

European Working Time
    Directive, 36
evaluation, 110–2
  conditions affecting, 112–3
  definition of, 111
  key area for achieving
    excellence, 123
  methodologies, 114–5
  strategies for, 113–4
  tools and techniques for,
    15–9
Every Child Matters (2005),
    35
evidence
  evaluating for practice,
    51–52
evidence base for practice, 66
evidence-based nursing, 102
evidence-based treatments, 51
excellence
  achieving, 21–4, 26
  definition of, 19–20
  drivers for, 33
  evaluation, 110–1
  framework for, 125
  in context of health and
    social care, 20–1
  inclusive approach, 52
  key areas for success, 123
  major considerations for,
    47
  potential value of, 24–6
  service user at centre of care,
    55
  through practice
    development, 120–7
  working towards, 122
excellence in practice
  background to, 1–2
Excellence in Practice
    Accreditation Scheme
    (EPAS), 91
  benchmarking in, 26
exercise
  promotion of, 38
experiences
  requirement for practice
    development, 12
expert patient groups, 57
expertness
  notions of, 53
External Reference Group, 52

facilitation
    importance of, 14–5
    practice development, 75
    requirement for practice
        development, 12
fees
    care providers' registration,
        87
    frameworks for sharing *see*
        networking
Freedom of Information Act
    2000, 38–9

General Medical Council, 40
General Social Care Council,
    40
governance
    domain of healthcare, 85–6
Griffiths Report, 34
guidance, 66

health
    standards for, 82
Health and Social Care
        (Community Health and
        Standards) Act, 2003
    main provisions of, 87
health care
    defining standards in, 84
    evaluation of, 110–2
    excellence in, 20–1
    media articles on, 47
    policy changes, 34–6
    rights in, 52
health care standards
    issues surrounding
        introduction for NHS,
        89–90
Health Development Agency,
    56
health education, 54–5
health living partnerships,
    54–5
health maintenance
    standards for, 53
Health of the Nation, The, 38
health professionals
    contract of employment,
        40–1
    duty of care, 40
    job descriptions, 41
Health Professions Council, 40

Health Service Executive
    South, 111
health services
    public policy, 32
Healthcare Commission (HC),
    23, 84, 89–90
healthcare services
    lack of confidence in, 1
    *Healthcare Standards: A
        Critique of the Department
        of Health's National
        Standards for the NHS*, 82
healthcare standards
    domains of, 85
    evaluation, 91–2
    interdependency with social
        care standards, 91
    new, 85–7
healthy eating
    promotion of, 38
heathcare standards
    existing systems compared,
        89–90
    high blood pressure *see*
        hypertension, 38
hospital
    average length of stay, 41
hypertension
    management of, 38

identity
    sense of, 64
impact assessment, 113
improvement
    shared working, 72
    Improving Working Lives, 124
indirect learning from practice,
    107
individuals
    attention required in
        practice development, 46
    influences on, 68
information
    care homes, 88
    greater access demanded, 1,
        39–40
    improving access to, 56–7
    requirement for practice
        development, 12
innovation
    comparative models for,
        63–64

for achieving excellence, 47
    requirement for practice
        development, 12
integrated governance
    aims of, 64–65
integrated service
    provision of, 46
Intensive Care Society (ICS), 99
intermediate care
    care homes, 88
International Council of
    Nurses (ICN), 103
interpersonal relationships
    factor defining
        professionalism, 96
intra-organisation
    attention required in
        practice development, 46
Investors in People (IiP), 23, 81,
    90–1

job descriptions
    health and social care
        professionals, 41
junior doctors
    hours of work, 36

knowledge
    types of and practice
        development, 11
knowledge of patient/client, 97

leadership
    practice development, 74–75
leadership awareness, 98
league tables, 37
learning organisation
    concept of, 60
legal, ethical and professional
    regulations, 66
life expectancy, 36
life-long learning (LLL), 41, 96
litigation
    increase in, 42
    threat of, 1
long-term conditions
    patient management, 36
longevity, 38–9

management
    practice development, 74–75
measurement, 126

media
  coverage of poor clinical
    practices, 39
  criticism by, 47
meeting needs
  care homes, 88
Mental Health Crisis
  Intervention Teams, 36
mentoring, 40
  definition of, 106–7
moral agency, 97
morbidity
  changes in patterns of, 38
mortality
  changes in patterns of, 38
motivation
  for achieving excellence, 47
motive
  requirement for practice
    development, 12
multi-professional
  collaboration
  practice development, 9

National Electronic Library for
  Health (NeLH), 39
National Health Service
  Litigation Authority
  (NHSLA), 23, 42, 84, 90
National Health Service (NHS)
  establishment of, 34
  founding principles, 49
  issues surrounding health
    and social care standards
    for, 89–90
  lack of confidence in, 82
  performance management
    in, 48–51
  targets in, 48–51
National Health Services Act
  1948, 34
National Institute for Health
  and Clinical Excellence
  (NIHCE), 51
  clinical governance and, 66
National Service Frameworks
  (NSFs), 48, 52–3
  networking, 57
needs assessment
  care homes, 88
net model
  task culture, 73

networking
  information, 56–7
  participation, 108–9
  sharing ad dissemination of
    practice, 107
  New NHS Modern and
    Dependable, The (1997),
    35
NHS National Patient Safety
  Agency (NPSA), 100
NHS Reviews Coordination
  Group, 90
no blame culture
  shared working, 72
non-statutory supervision,
  104–5
nurse agencies, 87
nurse consultants
  development of, 36
nurse practitioners
  development of, 36
nurses
  accountability, 40
Nursing and Midwifery
  Council, 40
Nursing Development Units
  (NDUs), 22–3
nursing research, 102–3

obesity
  concerns over, 39
  increased prevalence of, 38
older people
  care homes, 87
  Options for Excellence, 35
organisation
  attention required in
    practice development, 46
  composition of, 60
  importance of, 60–76
  influences on, 68
  working in, 124, 126
organisation of practice
  factor defining
    professionalism, 96
organisational accreditation
  schemes (OAS), 120–1
  defining, 79–80
  models and frameworks,
    81–2
  strengths and weaknesses of,
    82

organisational change
  care delivery, 36
organisational culture
  types of, 73
organisational theories
  deficiencies in, 62
organisational working, 25
  Our Health, Our Care, Our Say
    (2006), 35
Over View and Scrutiny
  Committees for Health, 32
ownership
  sense of, 64

participation, 35
partnership
  work based on, 55
partnership building, 35, 53
Patient Advice and Liaison
  Services, 32
Patient Advisory Liaison
  Services (PALS), 38
Patient and Public User
  Involvement Fora (PPI),
  32, 38
patient dependence
  increasing, 41
patient expectations, 36–8
patient focus
  domain of healthcare, 85–6
'patient journey'
  design of optimal, 55
patient management
  long-term conditions, 36
patient participation
  research, 102
patient stay
  length of, 41
patient-centeredness, 55, 57
patient/client expectations, 1
  Patients' Charter, The (1992),
  32, 37–8
perceptions
  for achieving excellence, 47
performance assessment, 113
performance management, 25,
  48–51, 125
person culture, 73
person/patient centredness
  practice development, 9
personal evaluation,
  66–7

planning
  centralisation of, 47
political norms
  for achieving excellence, 47
power culture, 73
practice development
  accreditation and, 22–4
  achieving excellence
    through, 120–7
  attributes associated with, 12
  background to, 1–2
  characteristics required for,
    12–3
  communication required for,
    9
  core themes, 27
  critical social theory, 10–1
  definition, 5
  critical reviews, 6–7
  developing teams, 63
  emancipatory, 73–4
  encouragement required for,
    12
  external influences, 3
  facilitating excellence, 2
  facilitation, 12, 75
  framework for, 8, 125
  historical overview, 2–3
  individual, 46
  information requirement
    for, 12
  ingredients for excellence in,
    75
  intra-organisation, 46
  leadership, 74–5
  management, 74–5
  multi-professional
    collaboration, 9
  networking, 107–9
  organisation, 46
  person/patient centredness
    of, 9
  qualities required for, 12–3
  skills required for, 13
  support required for, 12
  supra-organisational, 46
  targets, 4
  team work required for, 9
  transportation approach, 74
  types of knowledge and, 11
Practice Development Units
  (PDU), 22–3, 81

practice knowledge, 96
preceptorship
  definition of, 106–7
preventive medicine
  standards for, 53
procedures, 66
professional bodies, 40
professional conduct, 95
professional development, 104
professional fora
  networking, 57
professional judgement, 66
professional practice
  factors influencing, 96–7
professional regulation, 95
professional responsibility, 66
professionalism, 35
  accountability, 40
  factors defining, 96
professions
  reshaping for achieving
    excellence, 47
protocols, 66
public confidence, 39
public expectations, 36–8, 53
public health
  domain of healthcare, 85–7
  networking, 56
Public Patient Involvement, 39
public perceptions, 66
public policy
  health and social care
    services, 32, 34–6

qualities
  required for practice
    development, 12–3
Quality Circle, 63
quality improvement systems,
  125
Quality in the NHS (1998), 35
Qualpac system, 22

Raising the Standards see
  Patients' Charter
re-admission rates, 41
realistic expectations
  shared working, 72
recognition
  factor defining
    professionalism, 96

reflective ability
  factor defining
    professionalism, 96
reflective practice, 98
registration
  care providers, 87
regulatory management
  centralisation of, 47
rehabilitation
  stroke, 41
research, 51–52, 66
  barriers to, 102
  reasons for, 102
research awareness, 100–1
  strategy for, 101–3
reshaping profession
  for achieving excellence, 47
respect
  requirement for practice
    development, 12
responsive care
  domain of healthcare, 85–6
rights
  health care, 52
role culture, 73
role identification, 71
root cause analysis (RCA),
  99–100
Royal Bristol Infirmary Inquiry
  (2001), 39
Royal College of Nursing
  Dynamic Standard Setting
  System, 22
Royal Liverpool Children's
  Inquiry, 83

safety
  domain of healthcare, 85
saliency, 96
sanctions, 66
seamless service
  aim for, 54
  self development see
    professional development
self-awareness
  shared working, 72
service considerations
  for achieving excellence, 47
service delivery, 47
  influences on, 54
sexual health, 39
shared care approach, 36

shared governance, 65–6
shared learning, 72
shared working
  practical issues, 72
  relationships, 69–70
sharing
  information, 56–7
  key area for achieving
    excellence, 123
Shipman Inquiry (2005), 39
skills, 97
  required for practice
    development, 13
social care
  defining standards in, 85
  evaluation of, 110–2
  excellence in, 20–1
  media articles on, 47
Social Care Institute for
  Excellence (SCIE), 23, 87
social care professionals
  contract of employment,
    40–1
  duty of care, 40
  job descriptions, 41
social care services
  public policy, 32
social care standards
  application of, 90–1
  evaluation, 91–2
  existing systems compared,
    89–90
  interdependency with
    healthcare standards,
    91
  issues surrounding
    introduction for NHS,
    89–90
social model, 35–6
social norms
  for achieving excellence, 47
social services care
  excellence in, 21
  policy changes, 34–6
societal needs
  for achieving excellence,
    47
standards
  measuring, 23–4
  objectives of, 53
  Standards for Better Health,
    82

*Standards for Better Health:
  Heathcare Standards for
  Services under the NHS - a
  Consultation*, 85–7
*Standards for Critical Incident
  Reporting in Clinical Care*,
  99
standards of practice
  for achieving excellence, 47
statins
  prescribing, 38
statutory supervision, 104–5
stroke
  advances in care and
    rehabilitation, 41
  reducing incidence of, 38
Stroke Unit Trialists'
  Collaboration, 41
Stronger Local Voice, A, 55
supervision, 104–5
  shared working, 72
support
  requirement for practice
    development, 12
  support networks *see*
    networking
supportiveness
  requirement for practice
    development, 12
supra-organisation
  attention required in
    practice development, 46
SWOT analysis, 98–9

targets, 48–51
  setting, 49–50
task culture, 73
team building, 110
team development
  group phases, 70
  through role identification,
    71
team reflections
  shared working, 72
team responsibility, 66
Team Technology, 110
team working
  effective, 56
  individual contributions to,
    70–2
  issues in, 72
  key principles, 69–70

required for practice
  development, 9
  shared, 72
teams
  approaches, 71
techniques
  for advancing and
    evaluating practice, 15–9
technological advances, 1
temple model
  role culture, 73
time
  for achieving excellence, 47
tools
  for advancing and
    evaluating practice, 15–9
Total Quality Management
  (TQM), 22, 63, 79
training, 66
transportation approach
  practice development, 74
treatments
  evaluation of, 51
trial visits
  care homes, 88

United States
  practice development in, 3
updating knowledge and skills,
  66
user-focused care, 124
user-focused working
  definition of, 25

values, 62–65
  clarifying, 63
vision
  clarifying, 63
visioning, 62–65

waiting times, 37
web model
  power culture, 73
whistle blowing, 39
whole system thinking
  concept of, 60
working environments
  importance of, 67–9
Working for Patients (1989),
  34
working relationships
  shared, 69